This book is dedicated
to my wife Michelle,
the best PR person,
in the world

Mt. Baldy from saddle before South Mt. Hawkins

Mountain Bicycling in the San Gabriels

Robert Immler

Wilderness Press
Berkeley

Copyright © 1987 by Robert Immler
Photos by the author
Design by Thomas Winnett
Cover design by Larry Van Dyke
Maps by John Stockwell

Library of Congress Card Catalog Number 87-40203
International Standard Book Number 0-89997-078-8
Manufactured in the United States of America

Published by Wilderness Press
             2440 Bancroft Way
             Berkeley, CA 94704

     (415) 843-8080

     Write for free catalog

Library of Congress Cataloging-in-Publication Data

Immler, Robert.
   Mountain bicycling in the San Gabriels.

   Bibliography: p.
   Includes index.
   1. Bicycle touring--California--San Gabriel
Mountains--Guide-books. 2. San Gabriel Mountains
(Calif.)--Description and travel--Guide-books.
I. Title.
GV1045.5.C22S275 1987   917.94'93'0453   87-40203
ISBN 0-89997-078-8

Contents

Acknowledgements

I wish to thank U.S. Forest Service Ranger George Geer for his cooperation and encouragement; Jerry Tate, of the Bicycle Touring Committee of the Sierra Club's Angeles Chapter, for my first ride on a mountain bicycle and for introducing me to some beautiful areas; and the Bell Helmet Company, Angell & Breeze, Specialized Bicycle Components, Scott-Mathauser, and Olympic Mountain and Marine Products for providing equipment for me to evaluate. Without them I would not have discovered that every corner of the San Gabriels is a treasure.

R. I.
Altadena, California
July 1, 1987

Introduction

A Cyclist's History of the Angeles National Forest

The Angeles National Forest was California's First National Forest and only the second in the United States. On December 20, 1892, it was created by a proclamation of President Benjamin Harrison as the San Gabriel Timberland Reserve. On March 4, 1907, its name was changed to the San Gabriel National Forest, and it received its current name on August 1, 1908.

After two enormous fires of 1919 and 1924 destroyed over 200,000 acres of watershed, Rush Charlton, Supervisor of the Angeles Forest at the time, realized that the greatest obstacles to the control of fires were the inability to locate the fires and the difficulty of transporting the firefighters through the mountains. As a way to overcome these obstacles, a system of fire-lookout towers, firebreaks, and fireroads was built.

During the Great Hiking Era, which lasted into the 1930s, more and more people began to hike, ride horses, take the Mt. Lowe trolley and, in a few spots, drive cars into the San Gabriels. Resorts, campgrounds and trails were built to accommodate them.

There were several reasons for the end of the Great Hiking Era. One was the Depression-era construction of the Angeles Crest and Angeles Forest highways by CCC workers, which opened up the backcountry to automobiles. Why spend a day hiking to Strawberry Peak when you could drive to its base and then be on its summit in an hour or so?

A second reason was the devastating flood of 1938. It destroyed most of the resorts that had attracted so many hikers into the San Gabriels.

A third reason was that better roads and more reliable cars made the San Gabriels relatively less desirable by allowing outdoor enthusiasts to drive more often to the Sierra Nevada, where they could hike in such grand places as Yosemite.

1

Whatever the reasons for the end of the San Gabriels' Great Hiking Era, the opening up of the backcountry to cars and the increasing numbers of cars meant that more facilities got built and more dirt fireroads got constructed. Treacherous routes—e.g., the Cliff Trail—were replaced by safe routes—e.g., the Mueller Tunnel. Dirt roads were built to allow for the installation and repair of powerlines. And the abandoning of the Mt. Lowe Railway left a gently graded, cyclable road from Echo Mountain to Ye Alpine Tavern.

Today these dirt roads provide a fine network of travel for the mountain bicyclist.

Turn of the century off-road cyclists

First on the Dirt

I have always loved the San Gabriels, so when I took up cycling, I naturally began to head into the mountains. At first my mindset did not include the possibility of cycling in the mountains on dirt roads. I had ridden short distances on dirt roads on a conventional 10-speed, but it was always a "walking on a tightrope" experience. On dirt, the bike never felt comfortable. Then I learned of one cyclist who went up the Toll Road on a road bike—but even he returned from Mt. Wilson on the Angeles Crest Highway. And I also met another cyclist who pedalled up the Angeles Crest Highway on a heavy (steel fenders and lights) 3-speed and then went down the Toll Road. It was these two cyclists who made me realize the possibility of riding both up- and downhill on the dirt roads of the San Gabriels—if the appropriate bicycle was available.

Origins of the Mountain Bike

In the mid-1970s a second bike boom was underway. (The first had occurred during the Gay 90s.) Although lightweight, multi-geared European bikes were popular, the restoration of 1930–1950 American bikes, notably Schwinns, became a fad. One result was the manufacturing of a modern copy of these Schwinns. But their single speeds limited them to flat terrain, and earned them the names "beach cruisers" and "klunkers."

Cyclists in California's Marin county began trucking old Schwinns and their modern imitations to the tops of hills and riding them down fireroads.

Gradually, people began converting these klunkers to five speeds. Then someone made a copy of an old bike, but using modern, lightweight, European bicycle tubing for the frame. To this frame, they added lightweight aluminum wheels with knobby tires, ultra-low gearing developed for touring, brakes developed for tandem bicycles, and lighter copies of motorcycle handlebars and controls. The result: A bike that because of interest in cruisers and old bikes looked right. A bike that because of its upright handlebars was more comfortable to those who found dropped handlebars back-breaking. A bike whose tires allowed it to be ridden on dirt. A bike whose brakes allowed it to be ridden downhill for miles with the calipers applied. And a bike whose gearing allowed it to be ridden uphill.

For me, the mountain bicycle combines the best of the two worlds of cycling and hiking. It allows me to see the same beautiful country as the hiker, but its greater efficiency allows me to enjoy about twice as much scenery in the same amount of time.

Comparing road and off-road cycling, Chuck Slack-Elliott, writing in *Bicycling,* says that mountain bicycling offers "rarely photographed vistas and encounters with wildlife and history unmatched on most stretches of paved roads."

Mountain bikes are also known as ATB's, or all-terrain bikes, because they're almost as much at home on pavement as off. Only the higher rolling resistance of their knobby tires, the poorer aerodynamics of the rider's upright position, and their slightly greater weight combine to make them a little less efficient on the road than their road-racing cousins. But they make up for this by being easily able to take to the shoulder when a car decides to pass—just as the road narrows!

Furthermore, because they're equally at home on pavement, they eliminate the need for a car shuttle. As an example, one can hike up the Mt. Wilson Toll Road, walk on the Mt. Wilson Road to Eaton Saddle, and then descend the Mt. Lowe Road. Few do this, because it's a tough all-day hike, and usually it requires two cars— one left at the bottom of the Toll Road and one left at Sunset Ridge. On a mountain bike, if one starts early, it's possible to finish that same trip by early afternoon. And it's an easy, mostly downhill ride from Sunset Ridge to the start of the Toll Road.

Legality

Has the mountain bicycle been welcomed into the wildeness? In a word, NO!

Can the bicycle be *legally* ridden on the hiking trails of the San Gabriels? A map published by the Forest Service in 1982 prohibits bicycling on some trails. But the 1985 version mentions no such limitation. And signs, posted in late 1985, imply that it's legal to ride trails.

Bicycling is definitely illegal in wilderness areas, and NO BICYCLING signs are posted in the Devil's Canyon area near Chilao.

The road leading into Santa Anita Canyon from the Chantry Flats parking lot used to be posted NO BICYCLING. However, I was told by one Forest Service employee that this was an illegal sign posted by an equestrian-oriented, anti-cycling ranger. Now I find, in early 1987, that the sign has been removed.

As this book was nearing completion, I learned that there's a 99% chance that the bicycle will be banned from all National Scenic Trails. This would be done at the Federal level, and there is nothing that could be done locally to counteract it. The Pacific Crest Trail is the local National Scenic Trail that would be affected by this ban. The Gabrielino Trail, a National *Recreational* Trail, would be unaffected by this ruling, but bicycles could still be banned from it any time in the future.

To compound this confusion, signs prohibiting off-road vehicles are common. The mountain bicycle is definitely a vehicle, and it is designed to be ridden off-road. But these signs were erected before mountain bicycles existed by someone who did not consider bicycles to be vehicles. Therefore, these signs do not apply.

Even where bicycling on trails is legal, should you ride there?

The bicycling community is divided on this issue. Charles Kelly, writing in *Bicycling,* says that if you're on a trail ". . . you go slowly, making sure that you do not skid. Your tires smoothly glide over the ground. This way, you have less impact on the earth underneath than a hiker has."

The logic behind this idea is that the fat tires of the mountain bike have a surface-contact area equal to or greater than that of the hiking boot. Therefore, the impact of the cyclist is the same as or less than the impact of the hiker.

But I have found that in many conditions it is impossible to ride on trails without skidding a wheel. Therefore, when I meet conditions, either up- or downhill, where my skidding wheel would erode the trail, I dismount.

Others think that even this practice is not enough. Also writing in *Bicycling,* William Saunders says that we should not ". . . ride bicycles on hiking trails. Bike tires cut and erode the surface and cause it to wash out, a problem with which backpackers have had enough trouble without contributions by cyclists. Do not ride a bike over any sort of easily eroded surface or anywhere in a truly wild area. Stay on dirt roads . . . power-line cuts and other tracks where man already has made an ineradicable impact."

From my point of view, although the sound of knobby tires going over a leaf-covered trail is wonderful, I usually prefer to hike on trails and to ride on fireroads. Echo Mountain is a good example. It is less than 3 miles from my house, and I have hiked and cycled there many times. I much prefer to hike the Sam Merrill Trail rather than ride it. But the Mt. Lowe Fire Road I find boring to hike, and prefer to cycle up.

It surprised me when the first conflicts regarding the bicycle in the Angeles National Forest were not between cyclists and hikers, but between cyclists and equestrians. A reason for this conflict between equestrians and cyclists could be that the horse may recognize the cyclist not as a human but as some strange animal. Many people recommend that the cyclist, not only out of common courtesy but also for the cyclist's own safety, stop and dismount, or at least stop, until the horse is past.

I've never had a problem with horses when I've slowed to a crawl. And once, after obtaining permission, I safely passed a police posse of about 30 riders. But it was a conflict between equestrians and cyclists that led to the banning of bicycles from Eaton Canyon Park. The horse set saw this as a great victory. But Eaton Canyon is a county park, and bicycling was already illegal in most if not all county parks. The equestrians really wanted bicycles banned not just from Eaton Canyon Park but from the entire Toll Road. So far, the Forest Service has decided to remain neutral—although one ranger, who was riding a horse on a trail at the time, told me that he felt mountain bicycles were no more damaging to trails than horses are.

I have been hiking, and recently cycling, the Toll Road for about 30 years, and I can't remember ever seeing equestrians on it. Confirming my memory was a *Los Angeles Times* article about this problem entitled: "Riders Resist the Wheel." In it were the results of a Forest Service survey. In a period of one month, 57 bicycles used the road, but only 4 horses!

The *Altadena Weekly* also reported on the problem in an article with the headline "Sheriff Takes Steps Against Wild Bikers." ("Wild Bikers" refers to mountain cyclists, not the Hell's Angels.) The article mentioned that on certain weekends in March 1986 the Toll Road would be patrolled. On one of those weekends, I rode the Toll Road in order to meet and talk with any officers who would be patrolling. Leaving my house at 7:30 A.M., I found no officials on duty at the gate. As I rode toward Mt. Wilson, I took my own informal survey, asking each hiker or runner (there were no equestrians to be seen) if they had ever encountered any irresponsible mountain cyclists. Most of the hikers answered "No." One regular Toll Road runner said that although she had never been bothered by cyclists, she had been bothered by equestrians.

Then I did meet a hiker who said that his sister had been knocked down by a one of three adult cyclists, whom he frequently saw riding too fast down the Toll Road. I then noticed that there were three sets of fresh tire marks. They indicated that three cyclists had just come down and were sliding their rear wheels around the corners. I wondered if these were the same three cyclists who had caused a rider in the *Times* article to be bucked off her horse. Could it be that these three cyclists were responsible for all the bad publicity about mountain cyclists?

In the year-and-a-half of riding that it took to research this book, I saw no cyclists exhibiting the fast, out-of-control style known as "Gonzo." But I did see two equestrians running their horses wildly down the Arroyo.

Although it's now legal to cycle on most trails (especially since the Forest Service discovered that to get some Federal money, it must serve even cyclists), the morality of cycling on trails is debatable. It appears that in the future, it may become illegal to cycle not only on trails but also on some fireroads. I have ridden on trails in the past, and I plan to ride more trails in the future. But because Robinson's *Trails of the Angeles* already offers the cyclist an excellent guide to the system of trails in the San Gabriels and because of the semilegal status of riding on trails (trail riding may even be illegal by the time this book is in print), most of this book is devoted to riding on fireroads.

Sign at Eaton Canyon County Park

Equipment

I used a bicycle in the $400 range to research the trips for this book. After I changed its stock 1.75-inch combination street/off-road tires to 2.25-inch knobby tires, it was completely satisfactory.

Although my bike came equipped with a quick release seatpost, to allow the seat to be lowered when descending, it soon became tiring and impractical to stop and reajust the seatpost every time I began to descend or ascend. A clever solution to this problem is Breeze & Angell's Hite-Rite, a spring that attaches to the seatpost and to the seatpost clamp. When descending, you release the clamp and allow your body's weight to push the seat down. When climbing, you release the clamp and the spring pops the seat back to its normal position. I'm long-legged and found that their longer Xtra-Hite model was perfect for me.

Another clever device is Tailwind's Shoulder Holder, distributed by Specialized. It combines a shoulder strap, for carrying the bike over obstacles, with a small bag (just enough room for a tube, a patch kit, and a small crescent wrench).

On a bike that may sometimes be ridden for miles with the rear brakes applied, excellent brakes are a necessity. Most riders agree that Mathauser pads are well worth their extra cost.

I've been searching for almost 15 years for the perfect chain lubricant. Mountain bicycling makes the chain lubricant's job even more difficult by adding dirt and water to the elements to which the chain is exposed. Soaking a *clean* chain in melted wax helps, because unlike other lubricants wax does not attract dirt. However, since it does not seem to hold up well in wet conditions, and since the chain of a mountain bike may occasionally be completely immersed in water, wax as a lubricant would seem to be impractical. However, Olympic Mountain and Marine Products' Lube-Wax, makes it easy to relubricate the chain because the wax is in an aerosol can.

Hazards and Dangers

On one level I think off-road riding is less hazardous than riding on the road, because you are much less exposed to motor vehicles. However, you will probably fall more while riding on dirt, and each time you fall, you expose yourself to injury.

In over 40,000 miles of road cycling, I've had about half a dozen spills, none serious. I probably fell at least that many times in my first month of owning a mountain bike. Of course, it has to be safer to fall onto the dirt at 5 mph than to fall onto the asphalt at 20 mph.

BRAKES: When riding on pavement, the rear brakes don't have to be used much. The fronts do the stopping, the rears keep the back wheel from skidding in a panic stop. I had gotten in the habit of almost never using my rear brakes.

It took time to change this habit. Because on dirt, just the opposite is true: the rear brakes do most of the stopping. Aggressive application of the front brakes could put your front wheel in a rut and put you over the bars.

HELMETS: I strongly recommend wearing a good hard helmet. Unfortunately, many cyclists who would never think of diving head-first into the ground think nothing of subjecting themselves to the same risk by riding without a helmet.

Bell has responded to the mountain bicycle market by selling a V-1 Pro painted in camouflage colors. Bell sent me one to try, but I prefer my older Bell Tourlite because of its visor.

I wish I could say that I always wear my helmet. I have seen research which shows that in hot weather body temperature is no higher for the helmeted rider. But my forehead hasn't seen these data and it doesn't just sweat—it *leaks*. So much perspiration runs down my face that I'm unable to see. As a result, in hot weather I strap my helmet to the bike when climbing.

RATTLESNAKES: One hazard in the San Gabriels is the rattlesnake. But although I saw many deer, quail, other kinds of snakes, lizards, etc., in over 700 miles of riding to research this book, I saw only one rattlesnake. As usual, it let me know it was there. I was on a trail and couldn't ride around it. So I squirted the reptile with my water bottle until it backed out of my way. I did discover, however, that a twig hitting the spokes can make a good enough imitation of the rattler's sound to make my hair stand on end.

POISON OAK: A much more common hazard is poison oak, usually found only on lower-elevation rides. Mugwort, a silver-leaved companion plant to poison oak, generally grows nearby. I can spot mugwort more readily than poison oak and usually see it first. I have found that if I rub my skin with the mugwort leaf where I've made contact with poison oak, the oil from the poison oak is neutralized. It works for me, but I know others who say it doesn't work for them.

RIDING ALONE: Although I know riding alone is potentially dangerous, one great advantage of bicycling as a sport is that you can do it by yourself. Still, a major fear of mine is to have an accident and to be immobilized in a remote area. Therefore, I leave my intended route either on an answering machine, on a note left with my family, or a note left on the windshield of my car. In case the worst happens, I carry extra food, water, and a mylar survival blanket in my bike bag.

INSECTS: More annoying than hazardous are the numerous insects found in the summer. I consider insect repellent to be an absolute must. I once forgot to bring it along on a 35-mile ride, and whenever I stopped, I would be attacked, so except for one spot where it is usually windy enough to blow them away, I had to keep moving. The insects turned a normally enjoyable ride into a miserable ordeal.

EMERGENCIES: The new mountain cyclist may still have the "road-racing mindset" of never carrying an extra ounce on the bike, thinking that any emergency can be handled by plastic money, hitching a ride, phoning home, or phoning 911. For road-racers, if you "hit the wall," food and fluids are as close as the nearest liquor store. But in the wilderness the credit card is worthless, and few cars, fewer phones, and no liquor stores exist.

TOOLS: The number of tools I carry depends on the length of the trip. For short rides, of up to 4 or 5 miles from my car, home or a major road, I carry a pump, a patch kit, a spare tube, and a small crescent wrench in the Shoulder Holder. If something breaks, I can walk out. On longer trips, where I might be 15 miles from a road, I carry the above plus a second spare tube, a chain tool, allen wrenches, a screwdriver, and spare rear brake and derailleur cables.

Mountain Bicycling Regulations

In late 1985 Ranger George Geer posted the following Mountain Bicycling regulations throughout the Arroyo Seco District of the Angeles National Forest:

BICYCLISTS

OBSERVE THESE RULES

MAXIMUM SPEED 15 MPH

CONTROL SPEED AT ALL TIMES

ALWAYS YIELD RIGHT OF WAY

STAY ON ROADS & TRAILS

ALERT OTHERS OF YOUR PRESENCE

AVOID TRAILS WHEN MUDDY

The National Off-Road Bicycling Association (NORBA) has put together 10 regulations to promote mountain-bicycling safety, to educate the cyclist in minimal environmental impact, and to help counter anticycling propaganda:

Off-pavement bicycling can open exciting new horizons for you. In order to maximize the benefit of your adventure and maintain the quality of the experience for those who will follow you, we urge you to adopt this code as your own.

1. I will yield the right of way to other nonmotorized recreationists. I realize that people judge all cyclists by my actions.

2. I will slow down and use caution when approaching or overtaking another and will make my presence known well in advance.

3. I will maintain control of my speed at all times and will approach turns in anticipation of someone around the bend.

4. I will stay on designated trails to avoid trampling native vegetation and minimize potential erosion to trails by not using muddy trails or short-cutting switchbacks.

5. I will not disturb wildlife or livestock.

6. I will not litter. I will pack out what I pack in and pack out more than my share whenever possible.

7. I will respect public and private property, including trail-use signs, no-trespassing signs, and I will leave gates as I have found them.

8. I will always be self-sufficient and my destination objective and travel speed will be determined by my ability, my equipment, the terrain, [and] the present and potential weather conditions.

9. I will not travel solo when bikepacking in a remote area. I will leave word of my destination and when I plan to return.

10. I will observe the practice of minimum-impact bikepacking by, 'taking only pictures and memories, and leaving only waffle prints.'

In late 1986 the Forest Service began to put up a triangular, yellow sign that NORBA has adopted. It indicates that the hiker should yield the right of way to equestrians, and that the mountain cyclist should yield the right-of-way to both hikers and equestrians.

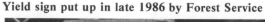

Yield sign put up in late 1986 by Forest Service

Trip Classifications

Trip distances: I measured the distances for the trips with a Cat-Eye 1000 Cyclometer. This device is adjustable to tire diameter only to the nearest inch, so I adjusted the readings to compensate for this inability to be more precise.

Time: Time includes rest stops, lunch stops and general exploring. I consider myself an average cyclist in terms of speed.

Elevation gain: Elevation gains were calculated from topographic maps. The figures are for total gains, not net.

Difficulty: Trips are classified according to time required and elevation gain. Easy trips take 1–2 hours and involve little climbing. Moderate trips take 3–4 hours and climb several thousand feet. Strenuous trips take 5–8 hours and may climb 5,000 feet.

Topo: This refers to the topographic map or maps that cover each trip. These can be purchased at many local backpacking shops, at map stores, or (without paying sales tax) at the Los Angeles Federal Building, Room 7638, 300 N. Los Angeles Street, Los Angeles.

Thomas Bros: For those trips that begin in a residential neighborhood, the start can be located on the indicated map and section of the *Los Angeles County Thomas Brothers' Map Book.*

Hundred Peaks: The Hundred Peaks Section of the Sierra Club's Angeles Chapter publishes a list of 270 peaks from the Southern Sierra to San Diego County. You must climb 25 of the peaks to become a member of the section; 20 of your 25 qualifying peaks can be climbed by using trips in this book. For a list of the peaks, send a S.A.S.E. and 50 cents to: Hundred Peaks Section Treasurer Tom Nealy, 6837 Vantage, North Hollywood, CA 91605.

Optional: Many trips have inadequate water supplies. In hot weather, I suggest taking twice your normal supply of water.

View from Echo Mountain on a clear day

Mountain Bicycling in the San Gabriels

1989 Update

Page 7. Before the last paragraph, add:

Of course, equestrian and hiking trails did not just appear one morning in the San Gabriels. They are all man-made. These days the Forest Service lacks the money for trail construction and maintenance, so all trail building and rebuilding is done by clubs—hiking clubs, equestrian clubs and, most recently, bicycling clubs.

The Mt. Wilson Mountain Bike club recently rebuilt the Sierra Crest trail, which parallels the Mt. Lowe road to the turnoff to Echo Mountain. They did the work with mountain bicycling in mind. Places that tires might erode were reinforced with wood, and places that encourage excessive speed were blocked to slow bicycles.

While trying it for the first time on a bicycle, I found my bare legs frequently touching poison oak. On foot you could get around it. On a bike I unavoidably rubbed against it several times. The route is more challenging and offers different views than the paved road. The only sign of any damage to the trail that could lead to erosion was from . . . a horse.

Page 8. Delete the fifth paragraph.

Page 9. After the first paragraph, add:

Recently the soft-shell helmet has become popular. It is very light and meets all safety requirements (at least for the first fall). But the off-road cyclist encounters one hazard more often than the road cyclist: rocks, and the soft-shell helmet offers no protection from penetration, a definite possibility should you fall on a sharp rock.

Page 13. At the bottom, add:

You may want to add to your drinking water one of the electrolyte-replacement fluids that are now on the market. They seem to increase one's endurance, and they mask the taste of any iodine tablets.

Pages 15–18, Trip 1:

At the top, the new distance is 7.50 miles. After the third paragraph, add:

You begin your journey at the corner of Ventura Ave. and Windsor St. in West Altadena. You can park in the paved lot immediately south of this intersection. There are two paved roads leading north into the canyon. The left (west) one descends into the parking lot of Cal Tech's Jet Propulsion Laboratory. You enter the road to the right (east) by riding around a locked yellow gate. Immediately, you will see a JPL ONLY sign. Ignore it; it should be on the other road.

Just past this sign is the only overlook of the trip. To your far left, you can see the Verdugo Hills. Just below you and across the canyon is what appears to be a small city. It is the Jet Propulsion Lab., from where all our space probes are controlled. Straight ahead is Brown Mountain.

Now delete the first two sentences of Paragraph 4 on p. 15. Then make the following changes in mileages for the rest of the trip:

old mileage	new mileage
0.14	0.60
0.29	0.75
0.42	0.88
0.79	1.25
1.10	1.56
1.35	1.81
1.49	1.93
1.58	2.04
1.74	2.20
1.85	2.31
2.23	2.69
2.54	3.00
2.90	3.36
3.29	3.75

Page 83. Below the text, add this note:

During the summer weekends of 1988, the operators of the Waterman Mountain Ski Lift began allowing mountain cyclists to take their bikes with them on the ski lift. The lift was open from 10 a.m. to 5 p.m. and you could buy an all-day pass for $10. This allowed you to get in as many as 6 or 7 runs in a day. From the top of the lift, you could either return directly to the Angeles Crest Highway on the lift-access road, or ride near the summit of Waterman and return on the more interesting and challenging hiking trail.

Page 79. Trip 20. Cooper Canyon is now off limits to cyclists, though the Burkhart trail is not.

The Trips

Trip 1

The Arroyo Seco

Distance: 6.58 miles
Time: 1½ hours
Elevation gain: 420 feet
Difficulty: Easy (Moderate if option to Angeles Crest is taken)
Topo: Pasadena
Thomas Bros: Map 19, section E4

A little over a hundred years ago, Bob Waterman and his bride visited the Arroyo Seco Canyon and spent their honeymoon hacking a trail that their horses could use. They returned and told a Los Angeles carpenter, Perry "Commodore" Switzer, about the beauty of the canyon. Switzer improved and expanded the trail and built Switzerland, the first resort in the San Gabriels.

Access into the canyon was by horse, stage or foot until the early 1920s, when the lower canyon was paved. Later, during the Depression, the construction of the Angeles Crest Highway allowed motorists to reach many parts of the upper canyon. Then the great flood of 1938 destroyed most of the paved road and the structures in the Arroyo.

Today, the Arroyo Seco Canyon is unknown, ignored or forgotten by the thousands of motorists who cross its lowest parts as they travel the 134 and 210 freeways. Yet a mountain bike allows the outdoor enthusiast to easily experience the beauty of both the canyon and the stream that carved it. An easy journey, Trip 1 is especially enjoyable early in the morning or later in the afternoon.

You begin your journey at 1220 feet in West Altadena at the end of Altadena Drive. Here you carry your bike over the barrier and descend on a dirt trail. Poison oak usually protrudes through the fence on your left. At mile 0.14 you turn right onto a paved road

15

and begin cycling into the canyon. The next 0.75 mile is paved, and occasionally you will share the road with Forest Service personnel and their families using it to drive to and from their residences.

At mile 0.29 you can hear water as it cascades over the stream's boulders and you ride across the spot where the stream from El Prieto Canyon joins the Arroyo. As the banks of the Arroyo's nearly-year-round stream become wooded, don't let the beauty distract you from the poison oak that is also in abundance. You now cross the first of the trip's 10 bridges, a substantial, concrete one.

At mile 0.42 a gradual bend in the stream creates a popular, though unofficial, picnic area. Another 0.1 mile finds you crossing a wooden bridge erected in 1939 by the Civilian Conservation Corps. Because the route is still paved, road bikes can use this part of the canyon, but the slots between the wooden planks make this a hazardous spot for them.

For a short distance, access to the water (used by the City of Pasadena) and to a grove of trees is prevented by fences. Then you cross the National Forest boundary and reach the junction of Forest Roads 2N70A and 2N66 (see trip 2). You take the left fork, 2N70A, and then the pavement ends and bicycle tracks in the sand immediately announce that you have encountered mountain-bicycle country.

At mile 0.79 you skirt the Forest Service residences, where a fountain has the only drinkable water on the trip. At mile 0.98 you cross the second wooden bridge and find an official picnic area, with table. At this spot, from 1914 until 1925, Theodore Syvertson had a store and six cabins. Today only a sign is left to remind us of Teddy's Outpost, once popular with hikers, equestrians and motorists.

At 1.10 miles another bridge crosses the stream, which has lots of water, even as late as September. You are now cycling essentially through a grove of birch trees on a road so sandy that a lack of traction, not steepness, will probably force you into your lowest gear.

At 1.35 miles from the start you ride across another concrete bridge and, to the west of the stream, you see a wall of granite, as beautiful as any in the Sierra. Then an additional 0.1 mile brings us to a bridge with a weight limit of 10 tons! Be careful: although built of steel, this bridge has a wooden surface with openings between the planks wide enough to catch narrow mountain-bike tires.

Next you can see—but not cross, because of a chain barrier with stop sign—the most impressive man-made structure left in the canyon. Although it has a sign that identifies it as the ELMER SMITH BRIDGE, the road on its far side has been washed away. Probably a victim of the 1938 flood, it leads nowhere.

Most of the year, you will ford the stream at 1.49 miles, and again just after taking the right fork at 1.58 miles. Taking the short path to the right just before the bridge at 1.74 miles can give you an idea of the resortlike nature of the canyon in the old days. Here you'll discover the foundations of several old cabins. One even has a rock love seat. A return to the road finds a wooden bridge, posted with only a 2-ton limit.

At 1.85 miles you reach the 1500-foot-elevation Gould Mesa campground, named for Will Gould, who owned land in this area in the early 20th Century. It's a pleasant but primitive campground (outhouses, but no water), which because of its inaccessibility by car is uncrowded, even on holiday weekends.

At the campground limits, you can turn left and take the road that climbs above Gould Mesa for another steep mile to the pavement of the Angeles Crest Highway, 2000 feet above sea level. Here your options are to use the Angeles Crest Highway for either a paved descent or for access to other unpaved roads (see Trip 5). Otherwise, at the campground limits you can continue straight, passing the Nino Picnic area and crossing two more bridges, until at 2.23 miles the canyon widens once more.

Here the wind blowing the leaves and the water rushing over the rocks usually drown out any sound from the Angeles Crest Highway, which can be seen 600 feet above you. The only sign of civilization is the occasional contrail that can be seen far above the hawks that sail on the canyon's thermals.

At 2.54 miles the road narrows almost to a trail, making further travel by mountain bike difficult. Those who like to keep their bikes clean and dry should return.

For others the next stretch involves more challenges: much walking of the bike, several stream fordings, and places where the bike must be carried across the stream. At 2.90 miles you will come to a massive concrete-and-stone structure. This is one of the few remaining sections of the old paved road. Leave your bike at the bottom and, using the rocks and roots for handholds, climb the 25 feet to its top. From there you can see that this was a major engineering accomplishment, not just a few inches of asphalt poured over existing ground.

On the bike again, you keep crossing and recrossing the stream several times until, at 1600 feet and 3.29 miles, you reach the Paul

Little Picnic area. This is a pleasant spot to end the trip. Modern picnic tables tastefully blend into the ruins of an old resort, making it a good place to rest before returning. Besides the table, it also has outhouses and a water fountain, which is unfortunately usually capped.

Author and friend crossing Arroyo Seco

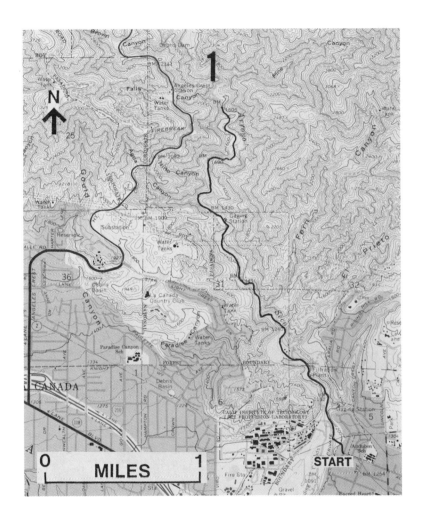

Trip 2

Brown Mountain

Distance: 12.85 miles
Time: 3 hours
Elevation gain: 1660 feet
Difficulty: Moderate (Strenuous if you hike to Brown Mountain)
Topo: Pasadena
Thomas Bros: Map 20, section A3
Note: Lug-sole boots and lock recommended, if you hike to Brown Mountain

This trip begins at 1440 feet, at the corner of Chaney Trail and Loma Alta Drive in Altadena, an area that used to be known for nursing plants into life and for nursing people back to health. This is a difficult, paved climb that takes you past reminders of Altadena's past: a commercial nursery on the left, and the pentagonal cabins of the one remaining sanitarium on the right. At 0.54 miles you climb one of the San Gabriels' steepest sections of paved road—but you are also rewarded for your effort by the first of this trip's great views of the San Gabriel Valley and beyond.

At 1.16 miles and 2080 feet, by the BROWN MTN. ROAD 1 sign, you turn left and descend into the canyon, first homesteaded in 1862 by Henry Millard. At the bottom of the hill, having descended to 1900 feet, you continue straight, past a locked gate, onto a dirt road. As you ride through the 5-site Millard Canyon Campground, you'll probably be able to hear the stream on your left and probably be able to notice the cabin on your right, one of several in Millard Canyon.

These and a few others, such as those in Big Santa Anita Canyon, are the only cabins that survived the 1938 flood. Many date from the 1910s, when they could be built on land leased from the Forest Service for as little as $15 a year.

Your water bottles should be filled here: it's the only source of drinking water on the trip. This campground is among the most pleasant in the San Gabriels. Few residents of the Los Angeles area are aware that this shaded campground, with a nearly-year-round stream, even exists. But its easy accessibility means it fills up early, sometimes even on winter weekends.

You may want to lock your bike here and hike the ¾ mile upstream to Millard Canyon Falls (see *Trails of the Angeles,* Trip 20). Along with the lovely falls, you'll see evidence of the canyon's mining past and a few more cabins.

Back on your bike, you ford the stream, turn left and begin climbing out of the canyon. Although this is mostly chaparral country, a few large oaks, occasional junipers, and a grove of young pine trees provide infrequent shade.

At 2.85 miles you reach El Prieto canyon. In 1854 Robert Owen, a former slave, came here seeking refuge from the prejudice he had found in Los Angeles. He built a cabin nearby, and by working in the valley became able to buy his family's freedom and bring them from Texas. He also supplied the Army with local wood and used the money from this endeavor to buy land in Los Angeles.

Because of him, this canyon used to be known as Negro Canyon, although today it is called El Prieto, which in Spanish means blackish or darkish.

Two other residents of the El Prieto Canyon area were Jason and Owen Brown, sons of John Brown, the famous Abolitionist. They arrived in 1884 and in 1885. As a tribute to their father, they wanted to name a mountain after him. They first attached the name to the summit we now know as Mount Lowe. This choice obviously didn't stick, but a later try for a slightly lower peak succeeded.

El Prieto's stream may have been the reason Owen chose this place as a homesite, and even now it creates a virtual oasis of oaks, pines and ferns. But the stream, which usually flows across the road, also gives rise to a great deal of poison oak.

This is a great ride, because on a clear day you see Santiago Peak in Orange County, the harbors of Long Beach and San Pedro, Palos Verdes, Santa Catalina and the Santa Monica Mountains. And if you do it in the late afternoon, the reflection of the sun off Santa Monica Bay can be a glorious, golden spectacle.

At 3.79 miles, at the junction with road 2N66, you continue right. It descends into the Arroyo Seco Canyon (see Trip 1). As you pedal, you can see the road to Mount Lukens on the other side of the canyon. Another 0.5 mile brings you to Fern Canyon. It has several oaks, with one huge example growing right in the middle of the road. Also here is a trough for horses, but cyclists must go thirsty.

Another few minutes of gradual climbing bring you to a spot where, with the 210 freeway far below, you can see across the Arroyo Seco Canyon to where the road to Mount Lukens leaves the Angeles Crest Highway. It is so far away that the sound of the wind and the songs of the birds drown out all but an occasional motorcycle.

After 6.19 miles and almost 2 hours, you reach the 2900-foot end of the Brown Mountain Road. Here you may want to lock your bike to the steel box and climb the 1.5-mile trail that ascends the steep ridge to your east to the 4466-foot summit.

After the hike, backtrack on your bike until at 9.88 miles you turn right onto the road marked by the sign ALTADENA 1. At 10.10 miles you arrive at an area where, today, people reside for the spot's serenity and beauty, probably the same reasons the Browns chose this area. Here you carry your bike over a locked gate and begin descending a paved road. At 10.19 miles, where the pavement turns left, you continue straight, uphill, on a dirt road. After 50 yards, just before reaching the electrical tower, you turn left onto a dirt trail. Because of the steepness and the erosion, you'll probably find yourself walking for a short distance. Then you ride beneath the electric tower, turn left, and continue riding until you come to a **Y** at the base of a small hill.

Here at 10.30 miles either leave your bike by a wooden rail that you can see across the left branch of the **Y** or you can push it up this branch of the trail for about 1 minute. At 10.35 miles, on the 1934-foot summit of Little Roundtop, is the grave of Owen Brown. A survivor of the Harper's Ferry raid, he spent his last years in this area with a price on his head.

Now you backtrack and turn right onto the paved road at 10.50 miles. This is a fast, steep descent with two potentially hazardous dips. At 11.10 miles you turn left onto Canyon Crest Road. As this road leaves the residential area, you find yourself above lower Millard Canyon. You can see an older home on the other side of the canyon build from native stones. As you ride the sweeping turn into the bottom of the canyon, you again cross Millard Stream, and then begin the climb up the other side.

At 12.25 miles turn right onto Lincoln Avenue and then almost immediately left onto Loma Alta Drive. At 12.85 miles you reach Chaney Trail and the start of the trip.

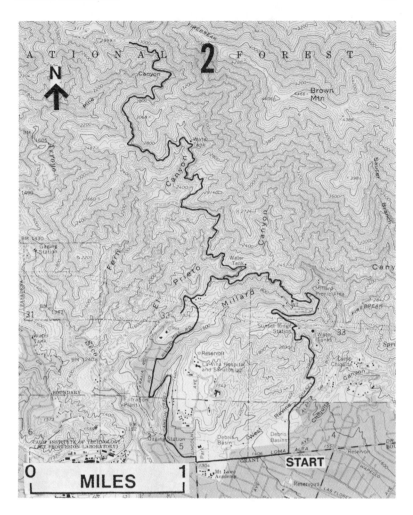

Trip 3

Echo Mountain

Distance: 6.62 miles
Time: 2 hours
Elevation gain: 1913 feet
Difficulty: Moderate
Topos: Mount Wilson, Pasadena
Thomas Bros: Map 20, section 2A

This ride begins at 2080 feet, at the top of Chaney Trail above Altadena, where there is a BROWN MOUNTAIN ROAD 1 MI sign. You don't go down the road into Millard Canyon, but instead take your bike around the gate and begin climbing up from the Sunset Ridge area. This area had, until they were destroyed in a windstorm, Camp Sierra (a resort) and several private cabins, famous for their views not only of the valley but also of the trolleys climbing up toward Ye Alpine Tavern. Even though the road is paved, it is a tough climb, and it would be even harder work except for the extremely low gears of the typical mountain bike.

Almost immediately, you pass a picnic table, a horse trough and a drinking fountain. Although recently it has worked, for years it was dry, and I wouldn't depend on it. At mile 0.90 Millard Canyon Falls can be seen below you. After about 45 minutes of hard climbing, at 2.40 miles and 3600 feet, you reach the turnoff to Echo Mountain. From this trailhead, you get good views not only of Altadena but also of Echo Mountain, now below you a little over ½ mile away. On the ridge to the left of Echo Mountain, what appears to be an old chimney is really the support for the telescope of the old Mt. Lowe Observatory.

Now you leave the pavement and begin cycling down a trail signed 12W14. This is the best-preserved section of the roadbed of the old Mount Lowe Railway. Many had dreamed of a railway into the San Gabriels, but it was not until an engineer, David Macpherson, and an investor, "Professor" Thaddeus Lowe, were brought together, that the dream became a reality. From its opening on July 4, 1893, until the floods of 1938 caused its closure, thousands rode from Los Angeles on streetcars, transferred to a steep incline railway in Rubio Canyon, and then completed their journey to Ye Alpine Tavern on the trolleys of the Mount Lowe Line.

When he had started the railway, Lowe had been financially independent. He gambled his entire fortune on the system. Unfortunately, it was never financially successful. By 1896 he was in debt, and 3 years later the courts sold the railway to pay off Lowe's creditors. It was acquired by Henry Huntington's Pacific Electric in 1902. Just 0.01 mile down the trail, eighty-some years later, you can still clearly see the results of the Pacific Electric's takeover. Here, and at several other former bridge sites around Las Flores Canyon, are the original rock foundations laid in the Lowe-Macpherson era, and the sturdier concrete foundations that were added as reinforcements by the Pacific Electric. Here also is the first of several places where you ride over some of the original ties.

At 3.15 miles you meet the Sam Merrill Trail coming up from Altadena, and at 3.19 miles you reach a water fountain and the start of the Castle Canyon Trail to Inspiration Point. At 3207 feet and 3.31 miles, after 1¾ hours, you reach the ruins of one of the great features of the Mount Lowe Railway.

Lowe's system had 4 hotels: the Rubio Pavilion at the bottom of the incline, the Echo Mountain House and the Chalet at the top of the incline, and Ye Alpine Tavern at the end of the line. Although all four have been demolished, the most complete ruins are found in the Echo Mountain area.

At one time this area was known as the White City. It featured two hotels, a small zoo (once managed by John Brown's son Jason), a museum, a huge searchlight and an observatory. Even though most evidence of these facilities has been destroyed, demolished or vandalized, you can still see almost 100-year-old proof that the mountain cyclist is not the first to use spoked wheels to explore the San Gabriels. Also spoked are the two pulleys and the old bullwheel that gripped the cable of the incline cars. After over 93 years of use and exposure to the elements, most of the fingers that held the cable still work perfectly.

Although the Forest Service has provided picnic tables, I, like many visitors to Echo Mountain, prefer to sit on the steps of the old hotel and, as I view the city below, try to imagine the scene in its prime.

Even though the actual railway was never popular enough with the public to make money, today the "fantasy" railway has a small but enthusiastic cult following. Several smaller books and one large volume have been written about the system. A local real-estate firm restored an old substation, and until early 1987 it housed not only their offices but also the Mt. Lowe Museum. One of the firm's brokers has "2 Mt. Lowe" as her personalized license plate. And I myself bought a charming, if run-down, house that features 160 feet of the system's former right-of-way in its backyard.

On the way back, you reach the Mt. Lowe Road at 4.20 miles. You can either turn left and in a fast five minutes ride back to the start or turn right and begin climbing toward Inspiration Point and Panorama Point, the destinations of Trip 4.

Los Angeles on a clear day from Echo Mountain

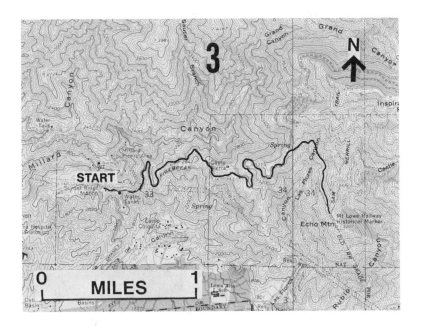

Trip 4

Inspiration Point

Distance: 14.51 miles
Time: 4 hours
Elevation gain: 3306 feet
Difficulty: Moderate
Topos: Mount Wilson, Pasadena
Thomas Bros: Map 20, section 2A

Like Trip 3, this ride begins at 2080 feet, at the top of Chaney Trail above Altadena, where there is a BROWN MOUNTAIN ROAD 1 MI sign. You don't go down the road into Millard Canyon, but follow the directions for Trip 3 until at 4.20 miles, upon returning to the Mt. Lowe Fireroad, you turn right and begin climbing.

At 4.23 miles a sign points out a rock formation, known as the Cape of Good Hope, and there is a photograph of what was the longest straight section of track on the Mt. Lowe Railway—an enormous 225 feet. The pavement ends at 4.26 miles.

Like the trail you have just ridden, this section was graded for use by electric streetcars. They are not the greatest hillclimbers, and as a result, although you're on dirt, this is especially easy climbing. You'll find yourself frequently in your middle chainwheel.

At 4.50 miles you reach the site of the Dawn Mine Station. Ore from the Dawn Mine, one of the San Gabriel's most successful gold mines, was brought from the mine by mules and loaded onto railway cars at this point. A sign here also points out Devil's Slide, an area of loose rocks that proved dangerous to many hikers.

At 5.04 miles you reach one of Macpherson's unexpected obstacles. He could not figure a way to reach the summit without increasing the grade beyond a tolerable level for the trolleys.

To get around this problem, he built the Circular Bridge. You can still see its foundations, almost 400 feet in diameter, off to the right. At 5.89 miles at an elevation of 4072 feet, you reach Granite

Gate. Here, the right-of-way had to be cut through solid granite. Although some blasting was used, most of the work was done by hand. Here also is another of the few remaining signs of the railway. Attached directly into the granite wall on your right is the last remaining support for the overhead trolley wires.

At 6.84 miles a sign on the left reads 12W18 SIERRA SADDLE. Just past this sign, on the hill above the right side of the road, you can see an old sighting tube from the Mt. Lowe days. The ones on Inspiration Point and Mt. Lowe have been restored, but this one looks original and is faintly labeled MT. LOWE.

At 6.87 miles, after 2¾ hours of climbing, you reach 4500-foot Crystal Springs, the former site of Ye Alpine Tavern. Today it is the location of the Mt. Lowe Trail Camp, which has 6 tables and stoves. There is a spring, but it is signed WATER UNSAFE TO DRINK. Presumably, this doesn't apply to the nearby drinking fountain. Although there doesn't appear to be much of the old resort left, an engraved Mt. Lowe Railway spoon was found here after a storm as recently as 1980.

I now understand more fully the reason for the railroad's financial failure, because when I ask elderly Altadena and Pasadena residents their opinion of the route, most reply that they never rode on it.

At 6.54 miles, after you leave the campground, with Mt. Wilson now visible, you turn right and head toward Inspiration Point. Professor Lowe's original plan was for Inspiration Point to be the end of the line. The right of way was graded, so the climb is easy, but Lowe had run out of money and the line was never finished beyond Crystal Springs.

Inspiration Point is reached at 7.33 miles after 3 hours of climbing. Old photos show a 5080 FEET sign, but modern topos list Inspiration Point as 4500 feet. A Pacific Electric constructed shelter has been removed, but most of the old sighting tubes remain. They have been restored and are aimed at local points of interest, a few of which did not exist in Professor Lowe's day. From here, on a clear day, Catalina Island, 60 miles away, is completely visible, and even on many smoggy days, the tops of its peaks poke up out of the inversion layer. If you find yourself cursing modern civilization when you can't see Catalina, remind yourself that even at the turn of the century, because of the haze, the conductor on the trolley was instructed to say that from here Catalina Island "may" be seen.

In 1915 a Mr. Zetterwall moved to the Alpine Tavern so that the clean air and water could improve his health. To support himself, he built the One Man and Mule Railway, the O M & M. Until 1935 Zetterwall charged tourists 35 cents to have Herbert, his mule, push them on a small trolley car from Inspiration Point to Panorama Point. Leaving Inspiration Point you continue on a dirt road that was the old O M & M right of way, until at 8.25 miles and 4400 feet you reach Panorama Point. To me it is more inspiring than Inspiration Point. From here, not confined by the walls of Castle Canyon, you can see Mt. Wilson, Mt. Harvard, much of the Toll Road, Orange County's Santiago Peak, Catalina Island, Santa Monica Bay, the Santa Monica Mountains, the Hollywood Hills, the Verdugo Hills, Santa Susana Pass and Mt. Lukens. Below you is Echo Mountain, and above and behind you is Mt. Lowe.

The water tank above you is used not only by the local lizard population as a spot to sun but also as a perfect place for the tired mountain cyclist to nap.

On the way back Inspiration Point is reached at 9.15 miles, the Mt. Lowe Road at 9.39 miles, and the remains of the Circular Bridge at 11.35 miles. At this spot, prepare yourself for the most spectacular downhill in the San Gabriels.

Only 10–12 minutes after leaving the Circular Bridge, you arrive at the start of the trip. Today Mt. Lowe and several street signs immortalize Professor Lowe, and Macpherson is remembered by a monument on Mount Lowe Drive in Altadena.

Old cable slot at Echo Mountain makes a good bike rack

Sighting tubes at Inspiration Point

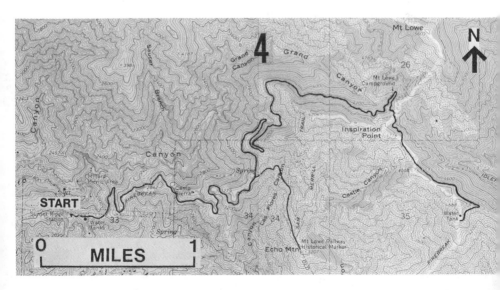

32

Trip 5

Mount Lukens

Distance: 17.54 miles
Time: 4½ hours
Elevation gain: 3834 feet
Difficulty: Moderate
Topo: Condor Peak, Pasadena
On the Hundred Peaks list
Optional: Double water

This trip begins at the 2240-foot Angeles Crest Station 3¼ miles up Angeles Crest Highway from La Canada. The water fountain in the grassy area by the parking lot is the only water on the trip.

You begin by riding up the dirt road that passes between the buildings of the ranger station. At 3.69 miles you come to a junction with the Earl Canyon Motorway. This much more difficult (much walking) route to Mt. Lukens begins in La Canada at the end of Palm Drive.

This junction has a concrete water tank with an almost flat top that is a favorite resting spot for both cyclists and hikers. This is a good place to have a snack and enjoy a view that includes the Brown Mountain Road, upper Arroyo Seco Canyon, and Mt. Gleason, the heavily wooded plateau in the distance. From this junction it is especially easy to see the steepness of the front range, which caused John Muir to comment, "I have never made the acquaintance of mountains more rigidly inaccessible."

After another 1.38 miles of climbing, the road becomes more nearly level. Big Tujunga Canyon Road, below you and to your right, goes over a beautifully arched concrete bridge as it passes just below the Big Tujunga Dam. At 6.54 miles you bear right and then begin the final climb. For several miles the summit has seemed to be "just around the next bend," an illusion that frustrates the strongest cyclist.

At 7.70 miles you finally reach the summit. Why do you find a grove of radio-transmission towers, not a grove of trees? Because this 5074-foot peak is not in the National Forest, but is the highest point in the City of Los Angeles. It was originally named "Sister Elsie," for a nun who ran an Indian orphanage. But in the 1920s the name was changed to honor Theodore Lukens, an Angeles National Forest supervisor. Although the road is signed MT. LUKENS, topographic maps show both names, and a bench marker on the top dated 1931 (after the name was changed to Mount Lukens) says SISTER ELSIE.

If you can imagine the many radio towers to be gone, the original beauty of this spot can still be appreciated. Today it offers excellent views of the San Fernando Valley and the rock formations of the Santa Susana Pass.

To return, you retrace your route. At 10.63 miles a choice of descent routes can be made. If you're tired, you can continue straight back the Mt. Lukens Road to the ranger station. If a little additional climbing won't bother you, you can turn left onto the road signed GRIZZLY RD.

To me, the latter is the prettier route, and its much lusher flora amazes me. At a junction at 12.65 miles you can take a short ride down the road to the right. It deadends in about 0.25 mile, but it's a lovely ride through a young forest of pines, planted to replace older relatives that were the victims of a fire.

Back at the junction you turn right. You'll have to do some climbing now, and at 13.15 miles you can see that you are now paralleling the Angeles Crest Highway, although about 500 feet above it.

Back down to 3000 feet, after 14.77 miles, you reach the Angeles Crest Highway. Turn right, and after 2.77 downhill miles you are again at the Angeles Crest Station. If you're still not tired, you can do sit-ups or pull-ups on the exercise equipment in the grassy area next to the parking lot!

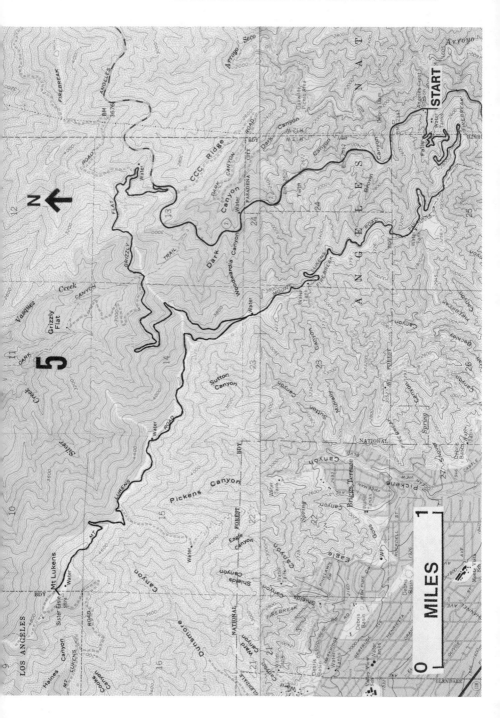

Trip 6

Josephine Peak

Distance: 8.08 miles
Time: 2¾ hours
Elevation gain: 1910 feet
Difficulty: Moderate
Topo: Condor Peak
On the Hundred Peaks list

This trip starts in front of the 3648-foot Clear Creek Ranger Station, at the junction of the Angeles Crest and Angeles Forest highways, 10 miles from La Canada.

You begin climbing the dirt road directly opposite the station by going around the locked gate. The road is signed JOSEPHINE RD. 2N64. There is little shade, so if you decide to do this ride in hot weather, an early morning or a late afternoon start is preferable.

In the spring, you can usually hear a stream that parallels the road until mile 0.33. Then at 1.48 miles Strawberry Peak looms ahead, and from its fruitlike shape it's easy to see how it was named.

For a few days in March of 1909, a runaway balloon put Strawberry Peak into the local headlines. A gas balloon carrying 7 men was tossed up into the mountains by an unexpected gust of wind. Faced with the choice of putting a hydrogen balloon down into an area that had a brush fire raging or allowing it to drift upwards into some clouds, the pilot chose the latter. Dressed for the low elevation and mild weather of Pasadena, the pilot and passengers found themselves in a snow storm at altitudes as high as 14,000 feet, until they were able to descend onto what turned out to be Strawberry Peak. Long before the construction of the Angeles Crest and Angeles Forest highways, they were really isolated. They spent the night around a fire and the next day were able to hike to the safety of the Colby Ranch.

After 2.50 miles of climbing, you reach the junction with the trail to Strawberry Peak. At 3.19 miles you take the left branch of the **Y**. Then at 3.85 miles you round a corner and see the summit for the first time. At 4.02 miles the fire road ends and a steep trail, which I was unable to ride, begins. In less than 100 feet you reach the 5558-foot summit.

Your 1¾ hours of climbing are rewarded by a view so magnificent that Joseph Lippencott, who used the peak as a triangulation point in an 1894 survey, named the peak after his wife. In 1937, because of increasing air pollution, the Mt. Lukens fire lookout tower was moved here. Today the tower is gone from here for the same reason, and only its foundations and an outhouse remain.

From the summit, which has a register, you can see Mt. Disappointment, Mt. Wilson, Mt. Lawlor, Strawberry Peak, the Mt. Gleason area, the waters of the Big Tujunga Dam and Mt. Lukens.

Since the road is no longer maintained, it is quite boulder-strewn and your return to the start will take almost an hour.

Climbing the road to Josephine Peak with snow still on the ground

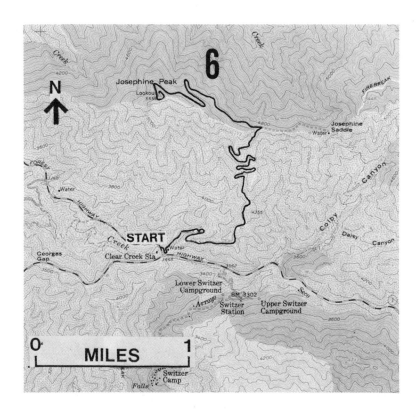

Trip 7

West Red Box Loop

Distance: 4.73 miles
Time: 1 hour
Elevation gain: 766 feet
Difficulty: Easy to moderate
Topo: Chilao Flat

This trip starts 12.4 miles from La Canada, just before the 4000-foot sign and milepost 36.09. You begin riding up the dirt road on the right (south) side of the highway and at mile 0.12 you take the uphill, left fork. The Angeles Crest Highway is steep and unsheltered, but this section of the Gabrielino Trail is moderately graded and you ride in the shade of a variety of trees, mostly oak. At mile 0.92 two especially huge evergreens have either grown together or one specimen has been split into two. There are good views of Strawberry Peak, which from this perspective bears little resemblance to its namesake, and of Josephine Peak. From this route, an old road that has eroded into a trail, you can hear traffic on the Angeles Crest Highway.

At 2.46 miles, as you near some Forest Service residences, you can hear the squawk box and see that the old trail has been closed off with a chain-link fence. The new route, which is now a narrow trail, goes to the left and drops before it abruptly ascends. In the last 10 yards you ride through the litter thrown down from a parking lot by those unaware of the trail below.

The 4666-foot Red Box parking lot is reached in 45 minutes after 2.62 miles. Here you can drink some water and use the restrooms, and then descend the Angeles Crest Highway back to your starting point, reached at 4.73 miles after one hour.

Riding the Red Box-Rincon Road on a Sierra Club-led trip

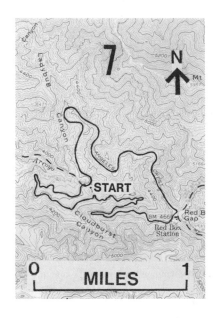

Trip 8

Rincon Road–Shortcut Canyon Loop

Distance: 24.54 miles
Time: 6 hours
Elevation gain: 2749 feet
Difficulty: Moderate
Topos: Chilao Flat, Mount Wilson
Optional: Double water

This ride begins at the Red Box Parking Lot, 14 miles from La Canada on the Angeles Crest Highway. At 4666 feet, the former ranger station has flush toilets and a drinking fountain.

From the parking lot you take the Mt. Wilson Road and immediately turn left onto Road 2N24, clearly marked by a sign as the REDBOX RINCON ROAD. Although this is a dirt road, it provides access for motor vehicles to two campgrounds. Cars, trucks and motorcycles are most common in the early mornings and late afternoons. Fortunately, they provide more dust than danger.

At mile 0.88, where a sign points to the Valley Forge and West Fork Campgrounds, you take the left fork, which becomes paved at 3.14 miles. At 3.21 miles the 3500-foot Valley Forge Campground, with 13 tables and 9 stoves, is reached.

At this site, beginning in 1922, Ernest and Cherie De Vore operated the Valley Forge Lodge. Advertised by its owners as "The Gateway to the Wild," the camp was dominated by a lodge constructed of native rocks. Other facilities included housekeeping cabins and a store. Hiking, fishing, and horseback riding were popular in this area, which had several streams with waterfalls. Here the great flood of 1938 produced almost complete destruction.

If you want to bypass the campground, bear left and continue paralleling the West Fork, which at 3.38 miles usually flows across the road, producing a slippery and potentially hazardous turn. Now the road begins to climb, until at 3.49 miles the pavement ends. Above you and to your right you can see Mt. Wilson. At 4.98 and again at 5.22 miles the stream may have to be forded again in the rainy season.

At 5.54 miles you reach the West Fork campground. Here the De Vores leased land from the Forest Service and started Camp West Fork. It had a store, cabins, tent cabins, a sawmill, vegetable gardens, an orchard and even a branch of the Los Angeles County Library. Camps such as West Fork were accessible only by foot or horseback and were either the final destination for visitors or places to stock up before venturing farther into the wilderness. In 1924 the De Vores mistakenly thought they were about to lose their lease at West Fork and began to direct most of their attention to their Valley Forge Lodge.

Today only ruins of the earlier resort remain; the only available supply for the cyclist is drinking water (your last source for the trip).

Leaving the 3100-foot campground, which has 7 tables and stoves, you immediately begin to climb out of the valley. You can take a break from the climb at 7.87 miles and see the road on the other side of the valley where you'll be climbing later in the day.

At 8.67 miles and 4040 feet, just after the road levels, you turn right and carry your bike around the locked gate. Now you're looking directly down Santa Anita Canyon. Far below you is the Chantry Flats parking lot. Below and beyond, you can see Arcadia, the San Gabriel Valley, and on a clear day, Catalina Island.

You continue this side trip until at 9.32 miles you reach Newcomb Pass at an elevation of 4115 feet. It was named for Louie Newcomb, whose trail of 1897 crossed this saddle as it connected Sierra Madre with the West Fork. After the two hours this part of the trip should have taken you, the shaded picnic tables in this area make a great place to relax and snack. A recent plaque serves as a memorial to a local runner who was blown off an icy trail during a fierce windstorm on January 12, 1985.

Returning to the Redbox-Rincon Road, reached at 9.97 miles, you continue right. At 10.33 miles you have the option of continuing straight (see Trip 27) or turning left at the junction signed SHORTCUT SADDLE. Carry your bike over the gate and begin the steep drop back into the valley.

Almost immediately, Cogswell Dam can be seen in the distance to the right. Then at a junction at 11.82 miles you continue left. At 13.33 miles a concrete bridge allows you to cross the West Fork once more. After about 3 hours of riding, the natural, nearly-year-round pools, at an elevation of 3200 feet, make a wonderful spot to relax and refuel before the climb back to the Angeles Crest Highway.

At one time, access into the wild backcountry was usually via Mt. Wilson. Then in 1897, Louie Newcomb built the shortcut Canyon Trail, bypassing Mt. Wilson. It eliminated about 5 miles from the route. You leave the West Fork by essentially following Newcomb's route.

At 14.91 miles you continue left, and at 19.45 miles and 4800 feet reach the Angeles Crest Highway, ending the unpaved part of the trip. (Note: If this trip is done in a clockwise direction, the Shortcut Road can be reached by going around the locked gate at milepost 43.30.) Here you turn left and use the pavement for your return to Redbox. This section of highway can be especially hazardous because, although heavily patrolled by both the Sheriff's Department and the California Highway Patrol, many motorcyclists and cars literally race along here.

Your start at Red Box is reached at 24.54 miles.

Author about to ride through stream in Millard Canyon

Michelle Immler

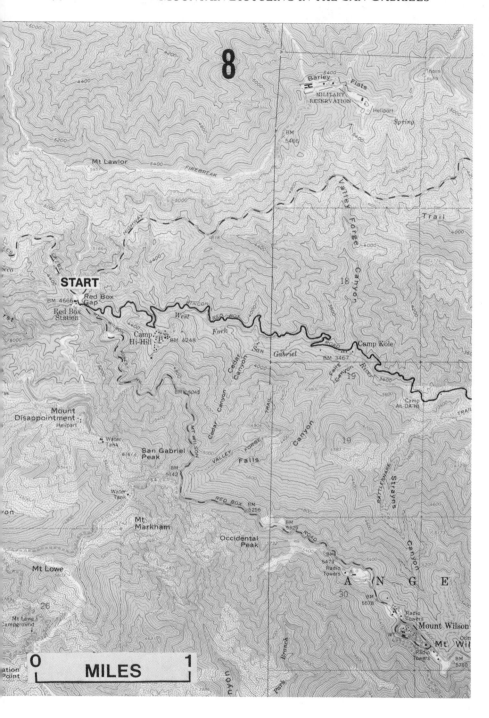

START

MILES

0   1

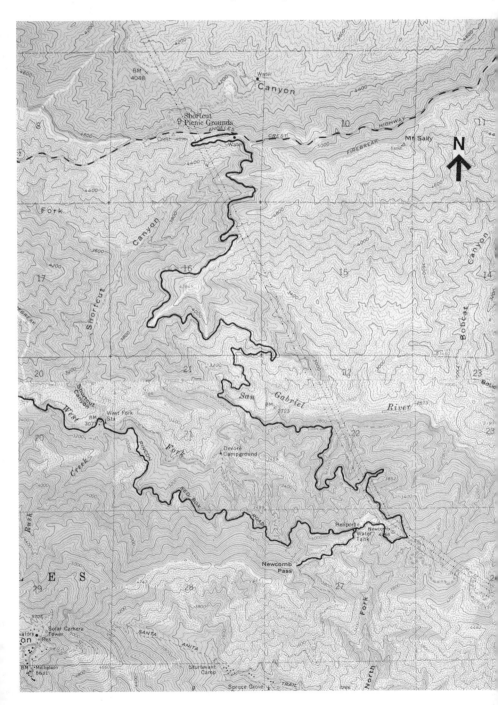

Trip 9

The Last Resort

Distance: 24.28 miles
Time: 6 hours
Elevation gain: 3576 feet
Difficulty: Moderate
Topos: Chilao Flat, Mount Wilson

This ride begins at the Red Box parking lot, 14 miles from La Canada on the Angeles Crest Highway. At 4666 feet, the former station has flush toilets and drinking fountains. From the parking lot, you take the Mt. Wilson Road and immediately turn left onto Road 2N24, clearly marked by a sign as the REDBOX RINCON ROAD. Follow the directions for Trip 8 to 4115-foot Newcomb Pass.

There are at least 3 apparent trails that leave Newcomb Pass. Take the one on the left that has the white steel post. At 12.04 miles you reach the junction with the trail to Mt. Wilson. Go right and uphill, toward Mt. Wilson. At 12.14 miles the trail goes left, but you go straight where the sign reads METHODIST CAMP. You have reached 3120-foot Sturtevant's Camp.

William Sturtevant discovered this spot in 1892 and opened a tent resort here a year later. The only way here was to hike in from Mt. Wilson. In 1895 Sturtevant began to improve and lengthen an alternate route up the Big Santa Anita Canyon. That year, when snow brought his work to an end, he established a winter work camp at the spot now known, because of this, as Winter Creek.

Sturtevant remodeled and reopened his camp in 1898, but beginning in 1906 others operated it. Sturtevant died in 1942 and the Methodist Church bought it in 1945. Today anyone can stay at the camp for as little as $13.75 per night (if you bring your own food), to as much as $40.35 per weekend (meals included). Advance reservations may be made by calling (818) 796-0157.

Even if the camp is closed, the picnic tables, the water fountain, and the turn of the century atmosphere make it an ideal destination.

At one time there were 20–30 resorts in the San Gabriels, five of them in this canyon alone. Among them were Roberts', Hoegee's, Martin's, Opid's, Valley Forge and Switzer's. Most were destroyed by the flood of 1938. Today few remain, and only Sturtevant's is open to the public.

At 13.29 miles, as you retrace your route to the Rincon Redbox Road, notice that the white dome of the Mt. Wilson Observatory can just be seen above another ridge. The Redbox Rincon Road is reached at 14.41 miles. Here you turn left, descend to the West Fork Campground and then climb back to Redbox, reached at 24.28 miles.

Sturtevant's camp

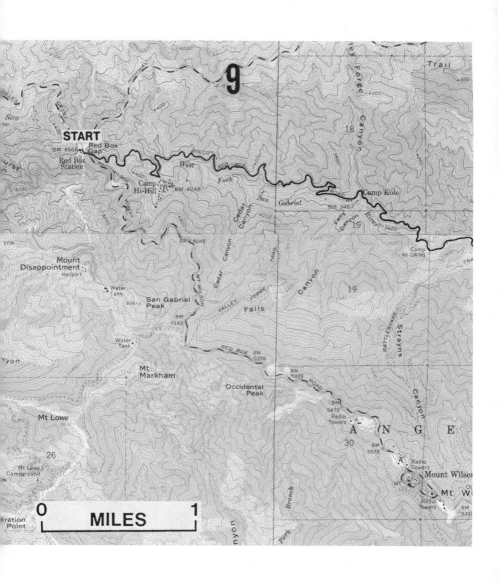

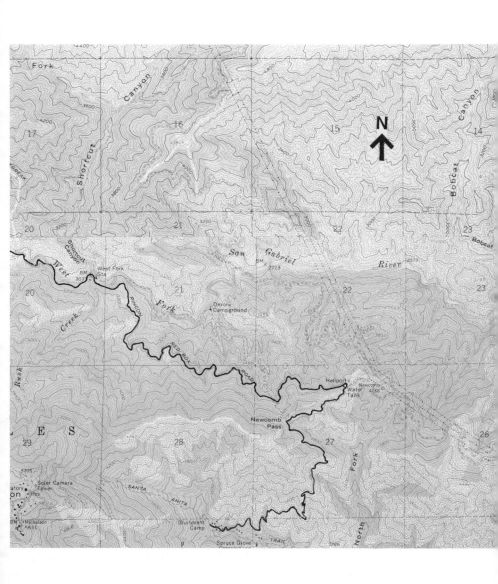

Trip 10

Henninger Flats

Distance: 5.48 miles
Time: 2 hours
Elevation gain: 1270 feet
Difficulty: Moderate
Topo: Mount Wilson
Thomas Bros: Map 20, section D4

This ride begins at 1300 feet at a gate opposite 2270 Pinecrest Drive in Altadena. After passing through the gate, you ride down the paved road, cross the bridge that spans lower Eaton Canyon, and begin climbing the dirt road.

You are now riding on a road originally conceived of by the Pasadena & Mount Wilson Toll Road Company in July 1889. The original goals were overly ambitious, and because the money ran out, the first "road" turned out to be a 4-foot-wide trail. It was opened in 1891, and the fee was 25 cents for hikers and 50 cents for equestrians.

When the 60-inch telescope was built on Mt. Wilson in 1907, the original trail was widened to a 10-foot road to allow the heavy mirror to be trucked to the top. The truck was a fascinating piece of machinery itself. A gasoline/electric hybrid, it cost $10,000, a fortune in those days. The first private automobile also went up in 1907, a trip described in the local paper as "foolhardy."

In 1912 the Toll Road was at last opened to the public. It enjoyed great popularity, although the owners claimed it never earned one cent in profit. Then competition from the free, faster Angeles Crest Highway doomed the Toll Road, and in 1936 it was turned over to the Forest Service.

At 2.74 miles, after one hour of climbing, you reach Henninger Flats. Today this is the location of the Spence D. Turner County Nursery. But in 1880 this was the homestead of William Henninger, a miner from California's Mother Lode. If your trip up the Toll Road has tired you, just imagine that Henninger's original trail came straight up from Eaton Canyon in about half the distance.

Today, 2500-foot Henninger Flats offer a good view of the valley, a museum, a nature trail, two Los Angeles County campgrounds, and an old fire tower that was on the Santa Monica Mountains' Castro Peak from 1925 until 1971.

Here you can either take the Toll Road back to the start or use the directions from Trip 11 to continue the climb to Mt. Wilson. On your return to Altadena, you should realize that this section of the Toll Road is heavily used by hikers. One reckless cyclist, causing one careless accident, could result in the banning of all cyclists from the Toll Road.

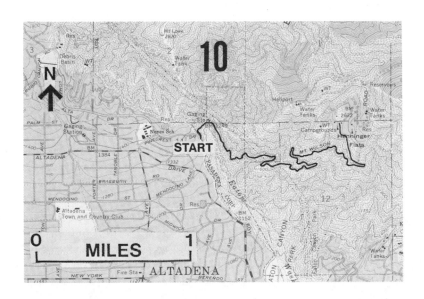

Trip 11

Mount Wilson

Distance: 18.92 miles
Time: 5–6 hours
Elevation gain: 4411 feet
Difficulty: Moderate
Topo: Mount Wilson
Thomas Bros: Map 20, section D4
On the Hundred Peaks list

Although easily reached by motor vehicle, Mt. Wilson is still a favorite destination of hikers, ultra-marathon runners, road cyclists and mountain cyclists.

To reach Mt. Wilson, you first ride to Henninger Flats (see Trip 10) and then take the road to the right of the nursery. It is signed MT. WILSON NO WATER NEXT 6½ MI. The first road to the right goes to the upper campground. At 3.60 miles you come to the turnoff to the Henninger Flats Heliport, and as you climb above Henninger Flats, you'll observe that the flora is noticeably greener.

At around 4.52 miles Mt. Wilson is seen for the first time and you leave the wooded area. For much of the rest of the trip, the route is unshaded, and the gnats and deer flies seem to be particularly annoying. But an area signed MT. FUJI nearly always has a refreshing breeze that blows them away even on the hottest day.

You again find some shade at 5.68 miles, and at 6.15 miles, after 2½ hours, you reach a ridge with the sign PT. GARYAL, MT. WILSON 3.5 MI. From this ridge, far from the cities below, the quiet allows the sounds of the wind and the wildlife to be heard.

At 7.56 miles you meet a trail that has come up from Santa Anita Canyon. From this junction Mt. Wilson looks to be just around the corner, but it is still 2 uphill miles away. From this spot, you can see a lush valley to the right, and beyond it Santiago Peak, Mt. San Antonio, and Mt. San Gorgonio.

At 8.08 miles you reach the side road to Mt. Harvard (see Trip

15). Then after a tough, though paved, last 20 yards (which may force the rider to stand up, even in the lowest gear), you reach the gate to the Mt. Wilson Road, at 9.10 miles after 4 hours.

Since Mt. Wilson can be seen from most of Southern California, it was a natural site for television transmission towers, and a grove of steel towers has sprouted from the ridge to the west of Mt. Wilson.

You reach 5710-foot Mt. Wilson by riding through the gates of Skyline Park. In the south end of the parking lot is a plaque to Benjamin Davis Wilson, erected by the Daughters of the American Revolution in 1935. The parking lot also offers good views of Mt. Harvard and the valley beyond.

To satisfy the needs of the many visitors who required food or a place to spend the night, The Mt. Wilson Toll Road Company built a hotel near the summit. When I was a boy, this hotel was a favorite destination for a Sunday drive. I remember the seemingly tame deer that were always around, the usually empty pool, and the great apple pie. I can still recall the smell of the fire that seemed to be always smoldering in the lobby's fireplace.

But the hotel was definitely in its declining years, and I remember hearing a dissatisfied customer coming out of the cafeteria, remarking, "That soup wouldn't make good dishwater." He was right, but it was a frigid winter morning, and even their "dishwater" tasted great.

In 1964 the Metromedia company purchased Mt. Wilson. They demolished the old hotel, built a concession stand, and in 1967 opened Skyline Park. Like so many operations in the San Gabriels, it was not a financial success, and it closed 8 years later.

For several years, access to Mt. Wilson was difficult. One could not enter from the paved road, but hikers coming up from Chantry Flats could exit the park through a one-way gate. Then, in 1979, Skyline Park was reopened by the Forest Service. The "modern rustic" concession stand and its porch offer good views of the valley and the surrounding mountains. The food is a little expensive, but where else can the mountain biker find any food at the end of a dirt road.

I always enjoy the ultra-marathon runners who eat there and seem to think that mountain bicycling is more difficult than running (for me, the opposite is true). Besides the concession stand, there are picnic tables, drinking water and restrooms.

To return to Altadena, you backtrack, reaching the start on Pinecrest Drive at 18.92 miles.

In the snow on Mt. Wilson

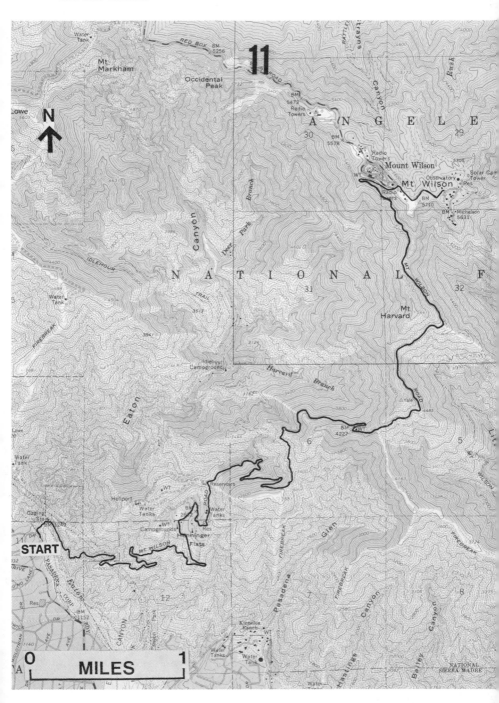

Trip 12

Toll Road–Mount Lowe Road Loop

Distance: 27.17 miles
Time: 6 hours
Elevation gain: 4500 feet
Difficulty: Moderate
Topos: Mount Wilson, Pasadena
Thomas Bros: Map 20, section D4
On the Hundred Peaks list

If you hike the San Gabriels, a loop consisting of a climb up the Toll Road to Mt. Wilson, a traverse to Eaton Saddle, and a descent on the Mt. Lowe Road is a full-day ordeal, usually requiring two cars—one at the bottom of Eaton Canyon and one at Sunset Ridge. But on a mountain bike, this route takes 30 minutes longer than a normal return from Mt. Wilson on the Toll Road. And because the bike can be easily ridden from Sunset Ridge to Pinecrest Drive, no car shuttle is required.

To do this route, you ride to Mt. Wilson (see Trip 11) and then as you leave Skyline Park you turn right and descend the paved Mt. Wilson Road, past the towers, to Eaton Saddle, at 9.74 miles, just before milepost 2.42. At the Saddle, after going around the gate at the end of the Mt. Lowe Road, you ride along precipitous upper Eaton Canyon and at 12.12 miles enter Mueller Tunnel. Bored in 1942, it replaced the dangerous Cliff Trail, traces of which can be seen on the outside of the tunnel. Your ride through the tunnel may be moist, because of seepage from springs or snow. The first ⅛ mile after the tunnel is rocky, and then at 15.27 miles you reach the turnoff to Inspiration Point (see Trip 4).

Inspiration Point, a worthwhile side trip, is reached at 16.47 miles. From there, you retrace your route back to the Mt. Lowe Road, reaching it at 17.67 miles. Then, just before you arrive at Granite Gate, a landmark on the old Mt. Lowe Railway, you can see a trolley-wire support, sticking out of the granite wall above the road. This is the last remaining support, of what must have been hundreds.

At 18.18 miles, at the former site of the Horseshoe Curve is a spectacular view of most of the Mt. Lowe Road. Then at 18.60 miles you reach the granite outcropping known as the Cape of Good Hope, and you say goodbye to the dirt road. Just before the gate at 21.07 miles is a water fountain that looks inviting but until recently was usually inoperative. After the gate, you go left, descend this steep, winding road, and turn left at the stop sign at Loma Alta Drive.

At the second stop sign, you angle off to the right onto Wapello Street. Then at Lake Avenue you turn right and descend to Altadena Drive. A left on Altadena Drive and another left at the first stop sign at Allen Avenue return you to the start on Pinecrest Drive.

Climbing the Mt. Wilson Toll Road

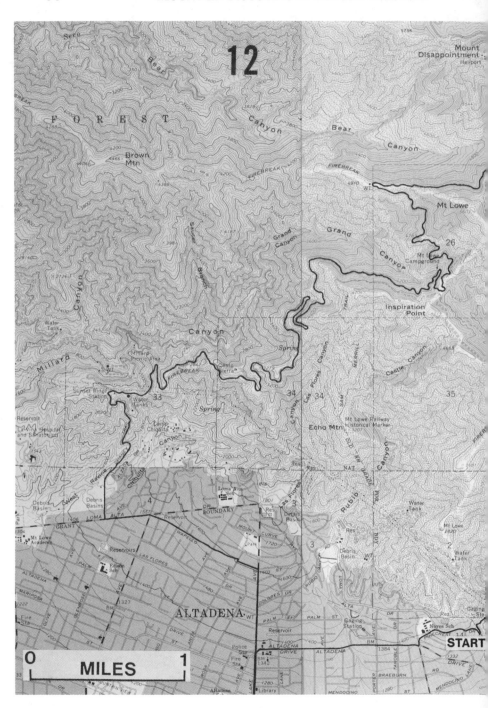

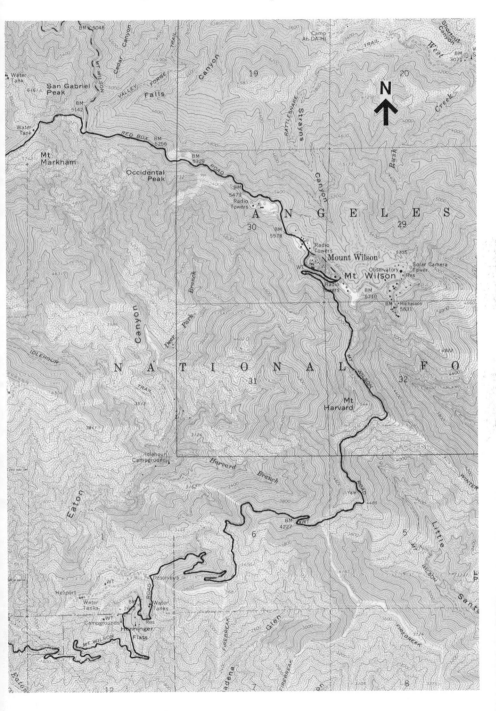

Trip 13

Sturtevant Falls

Distance: 3.62 miles
Time: 1¼ hours
Elevation gain: 760 feet
Difficulty: Easy
Topo: Mount Wilson
Thomas Bros: Map 20A, section F1

This trip begins at the 2200-foot Chantry Flats parking lot 5 miles north of Arcadia at the end of Santa Anita Avenue. You can drive to the parking lot, although the gorgeous ride up to Chantry Flats is a popular Southern California mountain training ride, and on a bike adds about 45 minutes.

Named after William Sturtevant (see Trip 9), this waterfall is the destination of one of the most popular short hikes in the San Gabriels. If you find competition for space with many hikers unpleasant, you may want to do this trip on a weekday. Its popularity can be judged from the fact that very late in the afternoon on a fall Tuesday, I shared the trail with 4 hikers, 2 other bikes, and a pack train. At the falls I was alone, but on a typical weekend there might be 10–15 people there at any given moment.

You begin the trip by riding around the gate below the parking lot that is signed GABRIELINO TRAIL. On the gate is a sign that has the word NO in large letters, the word **motorcycles** in small letters, and a vacant space that used to be occupied by the word **bicycles.** The mountain bicycle has just recently been allowed on this road. As you begin descending the steep, winding, narrow, paved road, be extremely careful! One accident could again eliminate bicycles from this beautiful canyon.

Hikers are not your only concern. Big Santa Anita Canyon is also home to the last pack train in the San Gabriels. It supplies the

Last pack train in the San Gabriels makes its way up to Chantry Flats from Big Santa Anita Canyon

cabins, supplies Sturtevant's Resort (see Trip 9), and carries out the canyon's trash. The pack animals are stabled at Chantry Flats, and their owners were unhappy when mountain bikes were allowed to use this road.

At 1560 feet and mile 0.61 the pavement ends. On your left is a small waterfall created by a debris dam. You can go over the pedestrian bridge to your right, although it is easier just to ride straight ahead through Winter Creek. On the other side of the creek, where today you find some pit toilets to handle this road's weekend crowds, is the site of the old Roberts' Camp. This was among the largest resorts in the San Gabriels. In its main two-story building and 24 cabins as many as 180 hikers could spend the night. It featured all the usual amenities plus a post office and county library branch. In its heyday 5,000 people once used its facilities on a single holiday weekend.

As you ride along the Big Santa Anita you will notice many cabins. Since all structures in the canyon were destroyed by the great flood, these have all be rebuilt since 1938.

This trip offers an excellent example of the difference in perspectives gained from hiking and cycling the same route. On foot, the paved downhill part is wide. On tires, it seems incredibly narrow. And once on the floor of the canyon, the hiker seldom notices the many small rocks that are easily stepped over, but for the cyclist each 6- or 8-inch stone becomes a challenge that takes complete concentration.

At 1.50 miles there is a well-signed junction. You want the trail straight ahead that parallels the stream. At 1.54 miles, the trail crosses the stream.

Here you may want to lock your bike to a tree and continue the final 0.33 mile on foot. I can say I've taken my bike to the falls, but I can't say I've ridden it there. At this first crossing, the hiker must carefully step from rock to slippery rock, but the mountain cyclist can pedal through the water.

At 1.71 miles, near a fallen log that spans the stream, you cross once more. Here the hiker has the advantage. The hiker needs only to balance himself as he goes across the log. The cyclist must also balance the bike. Once on the other side, you come to yet another pit toilet.

At 1.79 miles the stream is crossed a final time, and unless you're an observed trials champion, the bike definitely has to be carried here. The falls are reached at 2080 feet and 1.81 miles after 32 minutes of riding. In another 40 minutes you're back at the parking lot. In addition to the stables, a ranger station and a picnic area, Chantry Flats also has a snack bar.

Sturtevant's Falls

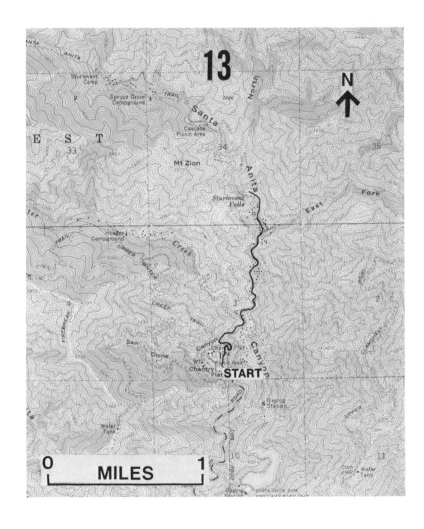

Trip 14

Mount Disappointment

Distance: 7.38 miles
Time: 1¾ hours
Elevation gain: 1328 feet
Difficulty: Moderate
Topos: Chilao Flat, Mount Wilson
On the Hundred Peaks list

Today, "Nike" is synonymous with a brand of athletic footwear, but in the Cold War 1950s, "Nike" meant a missile. In 1955 the Army flattened the tip of Mt. Disappointment to build a Nike Missile base. Although the Army only left a few traces of the old base's foundations here, it did leave behind a paved road. As a result, Mt. Disappointment is one of a handful of peaks in the San Gabriels with paved access.

You start at the 4666-foot Red Box parking lot, which has a drinking fountain and flush toilets. You begin riding up the Mt. Wilson Road, but just past milepost 0.39 you turn right onto a paved road and go around the locked gate.

As you gain altitude, not only do you find yourself riding among oaks and pines, but you will also enjoy great views of Strawberry and Josephine peaks. After only 0.77 mile you find yourself seeming to look down on Josephine Peak.

After 1.13 miles of easy climbing, you round the first hairpin turn of the trip to find Mt. Baldy and the entire eastern part of the San Gabriels lined up for your inspection. At the same curve, you get your first glimpse of the summit of your destination.

At 3.23 miles you ride through a gateless fence and make a sharp right turn before tackling the last several hundred challenging yards. After 3.69 miles and about 50 minutes of climbing, you reach the summit and can see how it got its name. In 1875, an Army survey team, needing a triangulation point, climbed this peak hoping its summit would be suitable. They were disappointed to find that nearby San Gabriel Peak was higher.

You'll find a register can among the rocks on the 5994-foot summit's southern edge. It might have been a disappointment for the old Army surveyors, but for the cyclist Mt. Disappointment offers great views in all directions except for the 40 degrees that San Gabriel Peak blocks.

Especially unusual from Mt. Disappointment is the view it offers of Mt. Lowe, the Mt. Lowe Road, and beautiful, shallow, wooded Bear Canyon, which lies between Mt. Disappointment and the Mt. Lowe Road.

On the way down, you may want to ride out onto the saddle between Mt. Disappointment and San Gabriel Peak. There you'll find more old foundations of what were once the barracks for the missile base.

With thoughts of Nike missiles in my head, I once climbed the galvanized metal tower protruding from the old foundation to see what was inside. I nearly fell off when I found myself staring at what I momentarily thought was the nose cone of a missile. It turned out to be only the conical end of a rain gauge!

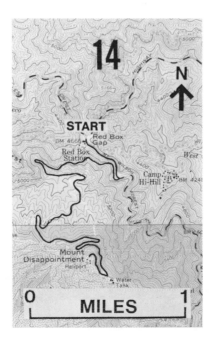

Trip 15

Mount Harvard

Distance: 3.06 miles
Time: ¾ hour
Elevation gain: 881 feet
Difficulty: Easy
Topo: Mount Wilson
On the Hundred Peaks list

This ride begins at the 5640-foot gate where the Toll Road meets the Mt. Wilson Road. Descend the Toll Road until at mile 0.98 you come to the Harvard-Wilson saddle. In the late 1800s, when Harvard University announced that a telescope was to be built on Mt. Wilson, the summit became a tourist attraction. Just as people today camp in the desert to watch the Space Shuttle land, many hiked to Mt. Wilson to see this 19th Century space explorer. Peter Stiel, a Pasadena man, realized that money could be made from providing them a place to spend the night, and he built some tent cabins on this saddle.

In 1891 Clarence Martin bought the resort from Stiel. He improved it, and for 14 years, until the much fancier Mt. Wilson Hotel opened, it was the best resort in the area. Today nothing is left of Martin's Camp except a deteriorating stone wall, and most of those who cycle, hike or run to Mt. Wilson are unaware of its existence.

At the saddle you take the road to the right, which soon becomes paved, although badly eroded. Twenty minutes and 1.43 miles after leaving Mt. Wilson, you reach the end of the road. You can leave your bike and walk up the ridge to the right (north) about 0.10 mile to the 5441-foot summit. In 1892 this summit was officially named Mt. Harvard to commemorate the visit of the president of that university.

Because Mt. Harvard is a favorite conditioning hike for those taking the Sierra Club's Basic Mountaineering Training Course, here, nailed to a log, is a metal summit register box marked BMTC. From the top you have good views of the trail from Chantry Flats, of the Toll Road, and of the Altadena/Pasadena area.

The return to Mt. Wilson is easy except for the extremely difficult last 20 yards before the gate.

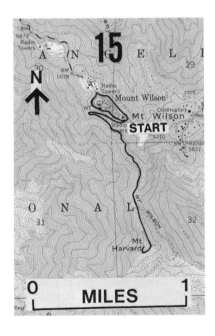

Trip 16

Mount Lowe

Distance: 8.22 miles
Time: 2 hours
Elevation gain: 937 feet
Difficulty: Moderate
Topo: Mount Wilson
On the Hundred Peaks list

This ride begins at the 4666-foot Red Box parking lot, 14 miles from La Canada on the Angeles Crest Highway. This former ranger station has flush toilets and a drinking fountain, the only source of water on the trip.

From here you cycle the Mt. Wilson Road to 5120-foot Eaton Saddle, just past milepost 2.42. There you carry your bike around the gate and ride along the sheer cliff that overlooks Eaton Canyon. Just before you enter the Mueller Tunnel, you can see the old hand rails fitted into the sheer rock wall. This treacherous route injured many hikers until this tunnel was built in 1942.

At 2.93 miles you take the trail to the left. It appears to go straight up, but after the first 10 feet it's mostly easy cycling. Riding along the lower flanks of Mt. Markham, you parallel the Mt. Lowe Fire Road below, with Mt. Disappointment and San Gabriel Peak to your right. Beautiful Bear Canyon is below you and Mt. Lukens is in the western distance.

At 3.53 miles you reach the saddle between Mt. Lowe and Mt. Markham. After another 10 minutes of climbing, the summit of Mt. Lowe is reached, at 4.11 miles. Here are the frame of a shelter (which looks too modern to be original), a bench, a hitching post, two beautifully weathered stumps, a flagpole identical to the one that once was on Inspiration Point, and several old sighting tubes. Left over from the Mt. Lowe Railway days, these point to Mt. Disappointment, Mt. Markham, San Gabriel Peak, Mt. Baldy, Mt.

Wilson, and Mt. Harvard. Located among the rocks at the base of the sighting tube for Mt. Harvard is the summit register. The 5603-foot peak also offers good views of Inspiration Point (almost 1000 feet below), the Mt. Lowe Fire Road, Altadena and Pasadena.

By retracing your route, you reach the start, after 2 hours, at 8.22 miles.

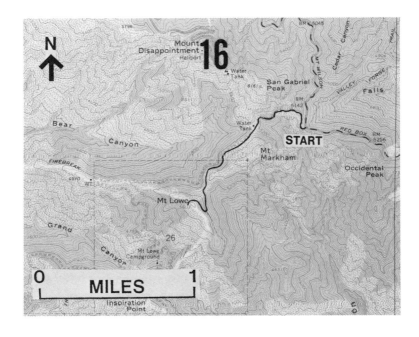

Trip 17

Vetter Mountain

Distance: 4.08 miles
Time: 1 hour
Elevation gain: 515 feet
Difficulty: Easy
Topo: Chilao Flat
On the Hundred Peaks list

This trip begins at the 5393-foot entrance to Charlton Flats, 23 miles from La Canada via the Angeles Crest Highway. You may be able to park even closer, but the ride through the Charlton flats area is too lovely to miss. As you cycle the road through Charlton Flats, you keep making left turns. You'll come to several gates. These may be open or closed, depending upon the season. Then at 1.32 miles you come to a gate that blocks access to a dirt road. This leads to 5908-foot Vetter Mountain after 2.04 miles and 7 minutes.

The Forest Service doesn't put fire lookouts where there isn't a good view. To the south you can see Mt. Wilson, San Gabriel Peak, Mt. Disappointment, Strawberry Peak, Josephine Peak, Pacifico Mountain, Waterman Mountain, Twin Peaks, Mt. Baldy and Monrovia Peak.

Although no longer used, this is one of the few remaining fire-lookout towers in the San Gabriels. Budget limitations have made having a lookout here 24 hours a day too expensive. And these days most of the fires in the San Gabriels are reported by one of the many aircraft that fly over the mountains. As a result, the Forest Service plans to move the Vetter Lookout to the Chilao Visitor Center so that its historical value may be saved and appreciated.

Climbing Vetter Mountain

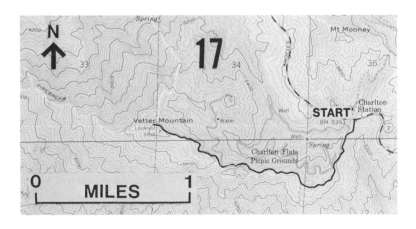

Trip 18

Devil Peak

Distance: 5.64 miles
Time: 1½ hours
Elevation gain: 917 feet
Difficulty: Moderate
Topos: Chilao Flat, Waterman Mountain
On the Hundred Peaks list

This trip begins outside 5393-foot Charlton Flats at milepost 47.54, near the apparently permanently closed restroom. You begin riding toward Chilao on the Crest highway but immediately turn right onto a paved road signed TRAILER DISPOSAL STATION. At the top of the paved loop, at mile 0.06, you take the dirt road signed ROUGH ROAD—though compared to many in this book it is quite smooth.

You continue riding through a dense forest of pines, until at mile 0.48 you come to a **T**. After a right turn, you notice some oak and to your left you have fine views of Waterman Mountain and Twin Peaks, separated from you by the still almost impenetrable Devils Canyon.

At mile 0.60 you come to a locked gate around which the bike can be easily ridden. Another 0.10 mile brings you to the short side road west to the small Stony Ridge Observatory. This was built in 1957 at an elevation of 5675 feet. Back on the main road, you descend until it ends at mile 0.88. From here your route is straight up the firebreak.

It's apparent from the tracks that at least some 4-wheel-drive vehicles have climbed or have attempted to climb this firebreak. But until I get 2-wheel-drive or a new set of legs, this is a section that requires pushing the bike.

The 5870-foot summit is reached at 1.07 miles. I had to walk all but the last few feet. In the distance are Mt. Baldy, Mt. San

Gorgonio and Santiago Peak, but the view is dominated by Monrovia Peak and Mt. Wilson.

On the way down it's easy to become disoriented. And you definitely don't want to ride into Devils Canyon, so at a junction you must take the trail that heads directly toward Mt. Disappointment.

Now, to make up for the effort required to reach the summit of Devil Peak, you can lower your saddle and enjoy one of the most thrilling unpaved descents in the San Gabriels. You reach the dirt road once more at 1.26 miles.

At 1.62 miles you again come to the **T**. But from this approach, it now has 3, not just 2, options. If you want to add another peak to your list, take the middle ridge, straight up, past the water tower. This difficult-but-ridable route reaches the summit of 5840-foot Mt. Mooney at 2.05 miles.

Back at the 5600-foot junction, you now go left. This great downhill stretch makes you think you're on the wrong road as it descends directly toward Devils Canyon. But just when you're worried that you're in for a long ride back up the hill, you turn toward Angeles Crest Highway, reaching it at 3.55 miles.

After a left onto the highway, you discover that, although you're still climbing, the low rolling resistance of the asphalt makes for an easy ascent. At milepost 48.00, after 3.90 miles of riding, the road's summit is reached. Then at 5.64 miles, after 1½ hours, you arrive back at Charlton Flats.

Stoney Ridge Observatory on the Devil Peak ride

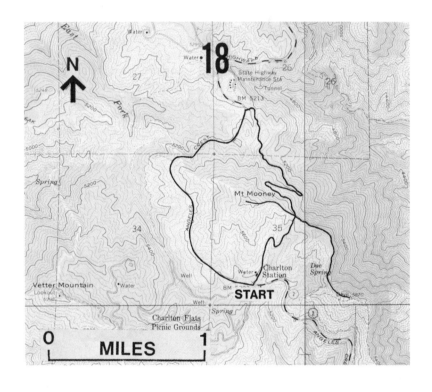

Trip 19

Chilao Loop

Distance: 11.40 miles
Time: 2½ hours
Elevation gain: 862 feet
Difficulty: Moderate
Topos: Chilao Flat, Waterman Mountain
On the Hundred Peaks list

This trip begins at the 5300-foot Chilao Visitor Center, 28 miles up the Angeles Crest Highway from La Canada. Today the Angeles Crest Highway makes Chilao an easy drive in a car or a moderately difficult ride on a bicycle. But in the 1860s and 1870s, this was remote country that the Mexican bandit Tiburcio Vasquez used as a hideout. Horses stolen from the San Gabriel and San Fernando valleys could be pastured here, and if the law was foolish enough to try to capture Vasquez, the boulders of the Mt. Hillyer region made a natural fort.

One of Vasquez's men, Jose Gonzales, was "hot" with a knife and hence was nicknamed chile pepper, or "Chileeyo." This was anglicized to Chilao.

Away from the sanctuary of the mountains, Vasquez was captured in Cahuenga Pass in 1874 and was hung in March of 1875. Then, with the area safe from human attackers, the plentiful deer and bear attracted hunters. Even grizzly bears were common enough to be considered a threat. Today, a different Chilao awaits the mountain cyclist. Weapons to ward off bandits or bears are no longer needed—although insect repellent may be a necessity.

At the Visitor Center you'll find exhibits that describe the area's biology and history. Several short hikes, especially popular with children, introduce the mountain novice to hiking. Leaving the Visitor Center, you follow signs that point to Chilao Campground. To the cyclist who rides through Chilao during its hot, dry summers, it's hard to believe that it's also a winter recreation area.

At 1.03 miles you turn right and follow the signs toward the Chilao Ranger Station. At 1.56 miles you pass the Chilao Mountain School and the Chilao Ranger Station, where there are water and a pay phone.

At 1.80 miles the pavement ends. Then at 1.87 miles you bear right following a sign that says NARROW ROAD 15 MPH. At 2.06 miles, on the hill to your right, is a Devils Postpile kind of rock formation. Next you ride through a short section of privately owned land, on which several cabins have been built. At 2.36 miles is the turn off to Loomis Ranch, the most distant from L.A. of the resorts of the Great Hiking Era. And at 2.46 miles you can see Vetter Mountain, Mt. Wilson, San Gabriel Peak, Mt. Disappointment, Strawberry Peak, Josephine Peak, Mt. Lukens, Roundtop, and Pacifico Mountain.

At 5759 feet, after 4.36 miles, you come to the paved Santa Clara Divide Road 2N17, onto which you turn right. Then at 4.67 miles, you leave the paved road and ride the trail on your right signed MT. HILLYER. It's only a mile to the summit, but it's the hardest mile of the trip. It's low gear most of the way, and in some places it's too sandy to ride, and in others, too steep.

After 1½ hours, you reach the 6162-foot summit at 5.55 miles. There is a summit register in the rock formation to the right. Two boulders in the area have man-made depressions, holes for grinding grain made by the first residents of the area, the Gabrielino Indians of the Shoshone Tribe.

At the rounded top beyond the summit, you take the trail that leads to the left and ride through the rock formations for which this area is known and among which Vasquez is supposed to have hidden from his pursuers. This is difficult but enjoyable riding. Most of it is downhill, but you still need the lowest gear for sections requiring power. From the footprints and the manure, you can see that this trail is popular with both hikers and equestrians, so be prepared to give them the right of way.

At 6.23 miles you enter 5700-foot, 25-space, waterless Horse Flats Campground. You ride through the campground and then at 6.77 miles you reach the paved main road. Here you turn right, and soon come to a vista commanding the range from Vetter Mountain to Strawberry Peak. At 8.19 miles a gap several miles away usually allows the desert to be seen. Below you and to your right, the Angeles Crest Highway can be seen winding through the forest.

Now you pass several church-operated camps. On a summer's day you don't realize how warm you are until you hear the screams of joy from the swimming pool of a camp run by the Mormons. Just before the Angeles Crest Highway is reached at 9.03 miles are restrooms and a drinking fountain.

At 10.35 miles a sign tells of the destruction by a 1924 fire. It contrasts this unplanted area's slow return with the comparatively quicker recovery of a planted area at the site of a Charlton Flats fire, five miles south.

At 11.01 miles you reach Newcomb Ranch, where you can purchase a snack at a cafe still run by relatives of Louis Newcomb. After 11.40 miles and 2½ hours you reach Chilao.

Rock Formation near Mt. Hillyer

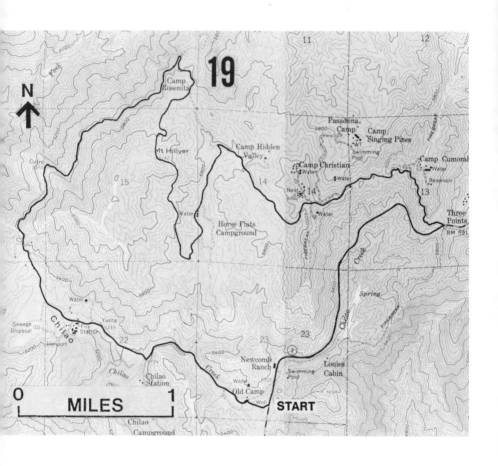

Trip 20

Cooper Canyon

Distance: 6.83 miles
Time: 2 hours
Elevation gain: 1298 feet
Difficulty: Easy to Moderate
Topo: Waterman Mountain

This trip begins at 7018-foot Cloudburst Summit just past milepost 57.04. You ride around the locked gate that blocks access to the dirt road on the northern (left) side of the Angeles Crest Highway. This gate cannot keep out motorcycles, so that, although illegal, their presence is a possibility to consider.

You quickly lose altitude among the Jeffrey pines and the incense-cedars, many of which have grown to monstrous sizes. This route was originally a logging road, and the hillside on your left shows the scars of clear-cutting. Then at 1.42 miles a sudden appearance of ferns on the floor of the forest gives a Northern California feel to the area and makes a great spot for a picnic. Or if you prefer tables, you can continue riding, until at 1.59 miles, and only about 20 minutes from the highway, you reach waterless, 6-space Cooper Canyon Trail Campground.

When the Indians roamed the San Gabriels, the males would camp in the Buckhorn area, but the women and children would stay in this region. Hence it used to be known as Squaw Camp.

Later two San Gabriel valley brothers, Tom and Ike Cooper, fell in love with this area. They would camp here when they hunted the abundant game of the late 1800s, and it is after them that Cooper Canyon and the Cooper Canyon Trail Camp are named.

There are two ways to return. You can retrace your route back to Cloudburst Summit, making for a trip of 3.18 miles in about 1 hour. Or you can continue through Cooper Canyon to Buckhorn. To go this latter route, you take the trail that at 1.75 miles narrows and crosses a small dribble of water from a spring, at 1.98 miles drops next to the creek, and at 2.34 miles has become a steep, rocky descent.

At 2.63 miles and 5720 feet, under an enormous cedar, you cross the stream for the first time and go up a hill. Then at the trail sign at 2.68 miles you turn right toward Buckhorn. The trail here is extremely steep and it narrows as it climbs. At 2.80 miles it descends and then crosses another stream.

This is rough going, requiring as much pushing as riding, and the stream can be heard 100 feet below us to our left. The trail is beautiful with ferns and fallen trees, and it's almost easier to walk than to ride.

At 3.88 miles you can hear and soon you can see the Angeles Crest Highway above you. Then at 4.12 miles you reach the parking lot for Burkhart Trail. From here, you continue along the dirt road to the extremely popular, 6300-foot, 40-space, Buckhorn Campground at 4.31 miles.

At one time a huge set of horns from a buck was nailed on a tree here, and because of that it is called Buckhorn. Today, even for the cyclist who chooses not to camp here, its drinking water relieves the thirst that this ride has induced. Here the road becomes paved, and at 4.52 miles you turn left, then follow the exit signs until the Angeles Crest Highway is reached at 4.88 miles. Now turn right onto the highway and reach Cloudburst Summit after 6.83 miles and 2 hours of riding.

On Mt. Disappointment

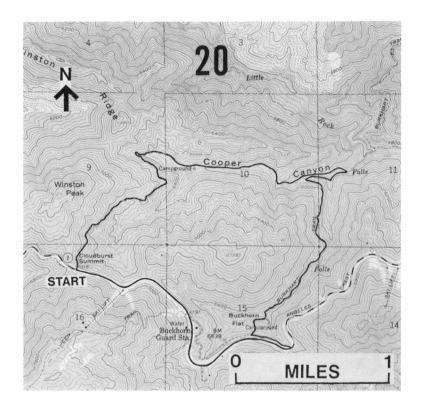

82

Trip 21

Waterman Mountain

Distance: 5.72 miles
Time: 2 hours
Elevation gain: 1247 feet
Difficulty: Moderate
Topo: Waterman Mountain
On the Hundred Peaks list

Take the Angeles Crest Highway ½ mile past the Mt. Waterman Ski Lift. The ride begins at 6791 feet at a locked fireroad on the right (south) side of the highway, just past milepost 58.07. It is signed: ROAD CLOSED TO ALL PUBLIC MOTOR VEHICLE TRAFFIC.

In 1889 Bob Waterman, his wife Elizabeth, and Commodore Switzer went across the San Gabriels to the desert and back. Enroute they climbed the tallest mountain in the area, believed Mrs. Waterman to be the first white woman on the top, and named the peak Lady Waterman Mountain. You begin your ride up what is known today simply as Waterman Mountain, by riding onto the fireroad. Immediately you cross a foot trail that also leads to Waterman's summit. You soon discover that because of the steepness of the road and the high altitude, Waterman may be a lady, but she is not gentle. Then at mile 0.46 the steepness of the road lessens and it is lined with Jeffrey pines, a few fir trees, and some granite outcroppings. At 1.21 miles the road steepens again, but nothing like the first 0.50 mile.

At 1.46 miles you turn a corner and have the first view of the desert to the north. At 1.85 miles a ski lift comes into view and you cross a minor dirt road that in the winter is used as a ski trail. More and more of the ski facilities come into view until at 1.92 miles you reach the main lift area.

Still popular with today's skiers, Waterman, the first ski lift in the San Gabriels, was built in the early 1940s by a cousin of Louis

Newcomb. Outside the lodge are a drinking fountain and picnic tables. Leaving this area you keep following the dirt road to the south as you head for higher points on the mountain. At 2.26 miles you take the road to the right, which has yellow SKI AREA BOUNDARY signs.

From the top of the ridge at 2.43 miles, much of the western and northern San Gabriels can be seen, along with the Antelope Valley, the Mojave Desert, and even the southern Sierra. But this is still not the summit of Waterman. To reach that, you keep riding on the road, until at the rain gauge at 2.55 miles you turn right onto a trail. By following this trail, you attain the actual 8038-foot summit of Waterman at 2.86 miles after 1½ hours of climbing.

Here on the stump of a lodgepole pine, among many large boulders, is a summit register placed on this mountain in 1924 by the Sierra Club. It shows an elevation of only 7752 feet. From this summit, home to numerous chipmunks, you look down onto most of the front range, with even Twin Peaks below you.

To return to the start, simply retrace your route. When descending the fire road, you get an excellent view of the section of Highway 39 that was destroyed by rock slides. After about 2 hours of riding, you reach the Angeles Crest Highway once more, at 5.72 miles.

Trip 22

Kratka Ridge

Distance: 1.83 miles
Time: 2 hours
Elevation gain: 715 feet
Difficulty: Moderate
Topo: Waterman Mountain
On the Hundred Peaks list

This ride begins at the 6800-foot entrance to Kratka Ridge ski area on the Angeles Crest Highway. Go around the locked gate just east of the Kratka Ski Lodge, and beyond the lodge, where there is a pay phone, you continue climbing west, above the highway. Then you turn left and begin climbing the ridge. This is a short but tough ascent that requires much walking.

At mile 0.32, at the upper tower of the lower ski lifts, you turn left and keep climbing. In about 50 minutes of mostly pushing the bike, you reach the upper lift towers. To reach the actual summit, leave your bike and climb to the top of the ridge behind the tower. From here it's an easy 50-yard walk to the highest spot on the ridge.

From Kratka's 7515-foot summit, you can see Waterman Mountain, Twin Peaks, and the section of Highway 39 made impassable by rock slides. There is a picnic table on the ridge and several more on the plateau below the lift tower. After 1.83 miles and a little over 2 hours, you're back at the start.

Roads in the ski areas are rated

Trip 23

South Mount Hawkins

Distance: 10.56 miles
Time: 4½ hours
Elevation gain: 2103 feet
Difficulty: Moderate
Topo: Crystal Lake
On the Hundred Peaks list

To reach the start, take Highway 39, 25 miles from Azusa to the Crystal Lake area. Follow signs to the campground, and park near the entrance to the campground by the Visitor Center and the store.

You begin the trip at 5680 feet, following the road that leads into the campground. At mile 0.32 the road widens into a large parking area. You want the road on the left (although all roads wind around and eventually end up at the right spot). At mile 0.62 you turn left onto a dirt road that has a sign indicating CAMPFIRES IN CAMPGROUNDS ONLY. These roads may or may not have locked gates, depending upon the time of year.

You begin climbing through pine and oak, until at 1.15 miles there is enough of a clearing to allow you to see Santiago Peak in the distance and to look down upon the front range of the San Gabriels and the San Gabriel Valley. At 1.48 miles you enter the 6300-foot Deer Flats Group Campground, with the last piped water and restrooms of the trip.

At 1.87 miles you turn right and ride around another locked gate onto the unmarked South Mt. Hawkins Road. After another 0.5 mile you ride through some trees whose enormous size is surprising for Southern California. And if you listen carefully, you can hear a brook that is piped underneath the road.

At 2.49 miles and 6600 feet you leave the shelter of the trees, cross a ribbon of water, and then see Mt. Wilson and Monrovia

Peak to the southwest. At 3.23 miles you cross an even smaller stream, fed by a spring just above the road.

At 3.69 miles you turn a corner and now can see the extremely serpentine San Gabriel Canyon Road below you. And above you, for the first time, you spot the top of South Mt. Hawkins, with its lookout. Another 1.25 miles of climbing bring you to the saddle between South and Middle Mt. Hawkins and you get your first view of frequently snowcapped Mt. San Antonio (Old Baldy), the highest peak in the San Gabriels.

At 5.08 miles the view to the south is actually better from the road than it will be from the summit. From this spot you can see what looks like most of the San Gabriel Canyon Road, the bodies of water formed by San Gabriel Dam and Morris Dam, the Glendora Mountain Road and the Glendora Ridge Road.

After 5.28 miles and 3 hours of climbing, you finally reach the 7783-foot summit. The fire-lookout tower was built in 1927, and in 1938 was moved from Mt. Islip to this location. Mt. Hawkins, Middle Hawkins and this peak were all named after Nellie Hawkins, an apparently beautiful and charming waitress at Cold-brook Camp's Squirrel Inn.

Because fire-lookout towers have been made obsolete by reports coming in from the many private, military and commercial aircraft that fly over the San Gabriels, the fate of this lookout tower is probably sealed.

On the return you reach the starting point at 10.56 miles after 4½ hours.

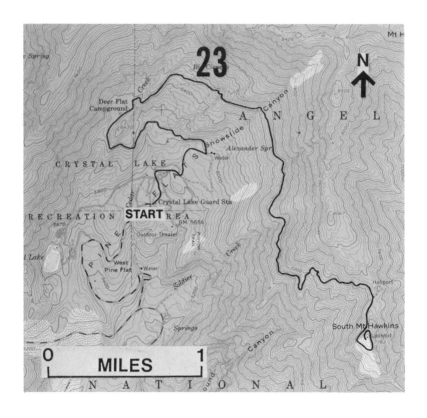

Trip 24

Sunset Peak

Distance: 8.34 miles
Time: 2½ hours
Elevation gain: 1373 feet
Difficulty: Moderate
Topo: Mount Baldy
On the Hundred Peaks list

This trip begins at a 4523-foot parking area on the Glendora Ridge Road, 1 mile southwest of the Mt. Baldy Road. Cross the road and take your bike around a gate blocking the dirt road. The first mile is a moderate climb through pine and oak that have survived an earlier fire. As you leave the trees, you can see the evidence of a more recent fire, and you have great views of the San Dimas Experimental Forest and beyond.

At 1.48 miles, after climbing to 5100 feet, you turn left. From here, the morning rider will encounter shade for most of the rest of the trip. At 1.85 miles Old Baldy can now be seen just peeking over West Baldy. For a short distance the road levels, and a higher gear can be engaged, but at 2.31 miles the road again steepens, forcing you to again go into your lowest gear. Now Mt. Wilson can be seen, and at 2.48 miles and 5500 feet the turnoff to Sunset Peak is reached.

After you turn left, there's a temptation to go up the steeper trail to the right, but because the main fire road soon deteriorates into a rock-and-boulder-strewn trail that I was unable to ride in many places, you should stay on the main road. It's challenging enough.

The 5796-foot summit is reached at 2.82 miles after 1¼ hours of climbing. There was once a fire-lookout tower here, but today only the old foundations are left. That's too bad because this old tower had some unusual history. It was built in 1914 and although it was on Lookout Peak, it was known as the Baldy Tower. It was moved here in 1927, but was destroyed by a fire in the late 1970s. Today, budget cutbacks and a change in policy toward lookout towers mean it will never be replaced.

From here on a clear day, you can see Mt. San Gorgonio, Santiago Peak, Palos Verdes and Catalina Island. As you leave the peak, the entire front range of the San Gabriels is spread out before you. At 3.16 miles you turn right, and then at 4.16 miles you have two options. You can turn right and return to the start by the same route, or to see slightly different terrain, you can ride straight ahead onto the unmaintained road. It is blocked by a bad slide at 4.62 miles, and you must walk and carry your bike about 50 feet to get over and around it. The small canyon you pass through on this way back has abundant wildlife, and in the spring the sides of the road are thick with purple lupine.

After 5.83 miles you ride around a gate and turn right onto Glendora Ridge Road. Road cyclists who train on this road have put up the HELL OF THE WEST sign here. You return to the start at 8.34 miles after 2½ total hours.

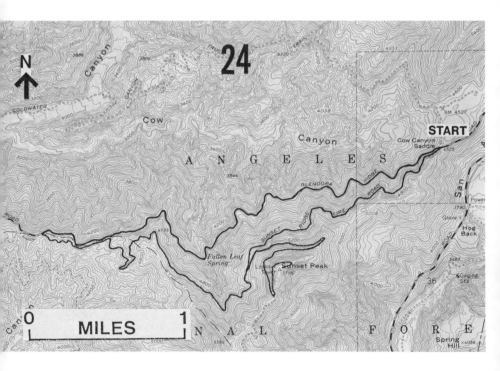

The trolleys are gone but a bicycle can still take you into the mountains.

Sturtevant's Camp. This structure is still in use, but only for storage.

The Arroyo Seco canyon

A Mt. Lowe car returning from Ye Alpine Tavern after a snowstorm

At the bottom of the Great Incline in Rubio Canyon

One of the Mt. Lowe trolleys near the Rubio Pavilion

Indian Day at Strain's Camp on Mt. Wilson, in August 1910

Trip 25

Thunder Mountain

Distance: 10.04 miles
Time: 4½ hours
Elevation gain: 2387 feet
Difficulty: Moderate
Topos: Mount San Antonio, Telegraph Peak
On the Hundred Peaks list

To reach the start, take the Mt. Baldy Road almost to its end. You start at 6200 feet at the dirt road across the highway and just uphill from the Movie Slope Restaurant.

Take your bike around the gate and begin climbing the paved but deteriorating road. At mile 0.32 you start to hear, at mile 0.41 you see, and at mile 0.59 you reach the side path to San Antonio Falls. Beyond the falls, the pavement ends and at mile 0.69 you ride over decomposed granite from the cliff on the left, which makes for extremely slippery going. As the road bends, you can see Sunset Peak and the electronic towers beyond it. At mile 0.92 the road allows almost no grip for the tires. I stopped and let air out of my rear tire to increase traction, and still I had to lean way back to put more weight on the rear wheel.

At 1.38 miles you hear running water and soon cross two streams that cascade down the canyon. Then you can see almost the entire ski lift, all the way up to the Baldy Notch Restaurant.

At 2.31 miles you cycle across another stream and then you find yourself riding next to the lift. This can be good or bad. It's good if you like being able to ride a bike up while others have to take the chair lift. It's frustrating if you're tired and would rather be on the lift. But just think of the money you're saving.

The route begins to switchback and you ride under the ski lift, then at 3.07 miles reach a junction. To reach Baldy Notch, you can take either the road straight ahead or the road to the left.

At 3.53 miles, after 1½ hours of climbing, you reach 7800-foot Baldy Notch Restaurant. In the off-season, the restaurant is open weekends and holidays. If the restaurant is closed, the picnic tables and drinking fountain still make a good place to rest, take on some food and water, and view the San Gabriel Valley.

After leaving the restaurant, you go 50 yards north and begin riding the road that takes off to the east. Soon you are at the actual notch and you get your first view of the Mojave Desert. Even when smog makes a view of the San Gabriel Valley hopeless, views of the desert can be excellent.

At 4.56 miles you come to a turn where Mt. Baldy is dramatically framed by some Jeffrey pines. Then you encounter a difficult section that will probably require some walking, and at 5.02 miles, after 3 hours of climbing, you reach the 8587-foot summit of Thunder Mountain. From here you can see the Glendora Ridge area to the south, the Mojave Desert as far as Muroc Dry Lake to the north, and Telegraph Peak and Cajon Pass to the east. From the summit, which has some lodgepole pines and firs, you can spot a green-roofed structure high on the slope to your west. It is the Sierra Club's San Antonio Ski Hut.

On the way down, you can attempt to do some of the expert ski runs on your mountain bike. The restaurant is reached at 6.63 miles. On the ascent you may not have noticed it, but at 9.19 miles is another view of the falls; from this perspective, three distinct falls can be seen. At 9.45 miles you pass the path to the falls, and at 10.04 miles you reach the Mt. Baldy Road after 4½ hours of cycling.

Mt. Baldy from the road to Thunder Mountain

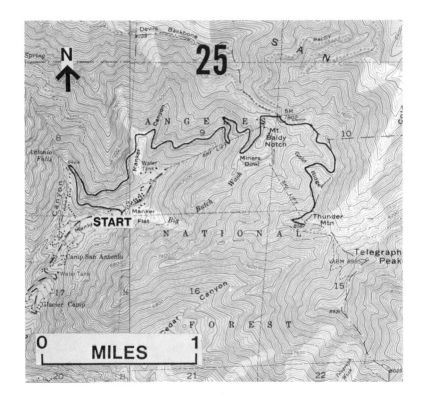

Trip 26

West Fork

Distance: 12.6 miles
Time: 2¼ hours
Elevation gain: 425 feet
Difficulty: Easy
Topos: Azusa, Glendora

This ride begins at a parking lot at a junction 11 miles north of Azusa on Highway 39, near milepost 27, where the West Fork San Gabriel River crosses under the road. This junction is signed SAN GABRIEL CANYON RD/WEST FORK RD.

Here you take your bike around the gate and begin riding up the paved, slightly uphill road. The parking lot and the West Fork Road near Highway 39 are heavily polluted with every type of garbage and trash, but by mile 0.33 the filth has disappeared, and by that time the sound of the West Fork has taken your mind off the debris. At 1.02 miles the stream forks, the northern branch being known as Bear Creek. You cross a bridge and continue to parallel the West Fork.

A second bridge is crossed at 1.65 miles, where a sign points out that from this point to Cogswell Dam the stream is stocked and maintained by the California Department of Fish & Game. Fish caught in this section of the West Fork must be returned to the stream. Because of this policy, you are able to see many trout from the bridge.

Although you are gaining altitude, it is so gradual that the knobbies are emitting their characteristic speed hum. After a few more bends in the road, you can see Twin Peaks straight ahead.

At 2.86 miles you ride across a stream that produces 2 small falls on the left, and at 3.72 miles another small trickle of water creates a magnificent 50-foot fall. Now you are going by some wide spots in the West Fork, the only location in the San Gabriels where

I've seen wild ducks with their families in tow. And just when you thought the best falls were behind you, another stream makes a 100-foot misty plunge down a mossy cliff.

At 4.52 miles you pass the only remaining cabin on the West Fork and then you go over a culvert with some small falls to the left. At 6.30 miles, after a little over 1 hour, you reach 2,000-foot-high Glenn Trail Camp. It has 6 spaces and pit toilets, but no water. The camp is shaded by sycamores, cottonwoods, and several varieties of planted pines, and in the spring, the field across the road is filled with Spanish Bloom.

The return to the San Gabriel Canyon Road is an easy coast.

The West Fork of the San Gabriel River

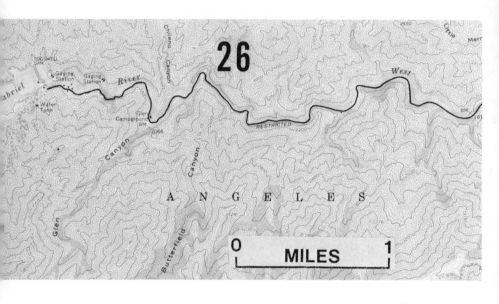

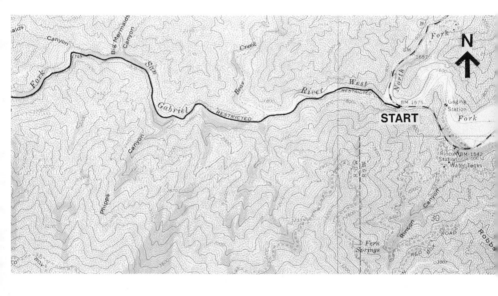

Trip 27

Monrovia Peak Loop

Distance: 31.60 miles
Time: 9 hours
Elevation gain: 3834 feet
Difficulty: Strenuous
Topos: Azusa, Glendora, Mount Wilson
Note: Double water

This ride begins at a junction 11 miles north of Azusa on Highway 39, near milepost 27, where the West Fork San Gabriel River crosses under the road. The junction is signed SAN GABRIEL CANYON RD/WEST FORK RD.

Follow the directions for Trip 26 to 2000-foot Glenn Trail Camp. Continue riding upstream until at 7.15 miles you have to work to get you and your bike to the top of 270-foot Cogswell Dam. Originally called San Gabriel Dam No. 2, it was finished in 1933 and renamed in 1935 to honor Prescott Cogswell, a Los Angeles County Supervisor known locally as the father of flood control. Water can usually be obtained from a faucet near the caretakers' residences. At 7.87 miles you may want to descend and to cross the dam, but instead you turn left and keep climbing. At 8.00 miles you leave asphalt, with the blue waters of the Cogswell below you. And since you're now out of the canyon, you have your first view of Mt. Wilson in the distance.

After a steady climb of 3½ hours, you reach a gate at 13.74 miles and 3960 feet. From here you could go left and begin the climb towards Monrovia Peak. Instead, I suggest turning right and heading to the picnic tables of Newcomb Pass for a well-deserved rest.

If you follow this suggestion, just past the signed TUMBLER SHOOTING AREA at 15.17 miles, where a water tower is marked NEWCOMB SADDLE, you will go around the gate on the left side of the road. At 15.80 miles you reach Newcomb Pass, at an elevation of 4115 feet. Here a bronze plaque honors Herman Kuhn, who in the terrible wind conditions of January 12, 1985, was running in the San Gabriels. That day, I turned back when attempting to hike to Inspiration Point for my 40th birthday. Kuhn did not turn back, and he was blown off an icy trail to his death.

Backtracking, you reach the Rincon Road at 16.40 miles. Turn right, and after passing the gate to the West Fork Road, you reach the gated Clamshell Road at 20.69 miles. Since you're this close, you may want to take a side trip to Rankin and Monrovia peaks. To do this, turn right onto the signed CLAMSHELL ROAD. At 22.11 miles, after you come into a clearing with the trunk of a burned tree on your left, turn left onto a barely perceptible trail. At once this becomes a ridable road. In 0.10 mile you turn left and begin climbing the ridge. For me this was unridable, and I had to push and carry the bike to the top.

5290-foot Rankin Peak is reached at 22.52 miles. Here (where from comments in the summit register you can see that most people think they have reached Monrovia Peak) are a flagpole and both bronze and marble markers honoring the Reverend Edward Rankin. The next peak on the ridge beyond you is 5409-foot Monrovia Peak, reached at 23.07 miles.

Backtracking, you reach the Rincon Road at 25.45 miles, and the summit of the Rincon Road, on the northern slope of Monrovia Peak, at 25.98 miles, after 8 hours. On the way down to Highway 39, you turn left at 26.57 miles and then at 29.70 miles you reach the turnoff to Pine Mountain. Here you turn right and continue your descent.

Although Highway 39 is easily spotted, the West Fork cannot be seen. The steep canyon walls hide it, even though it is now almost directly below you. This downhill, through lupine and Spanish Bloom, is extremely steep, leading one to imagine that coming up this way must be a real workout.

After turning left on Highway 39, you reach the start almost immediately, after 31.60 miles and over 9 hours.

Mt. Wilson from the road to Monrovia Peak

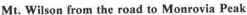

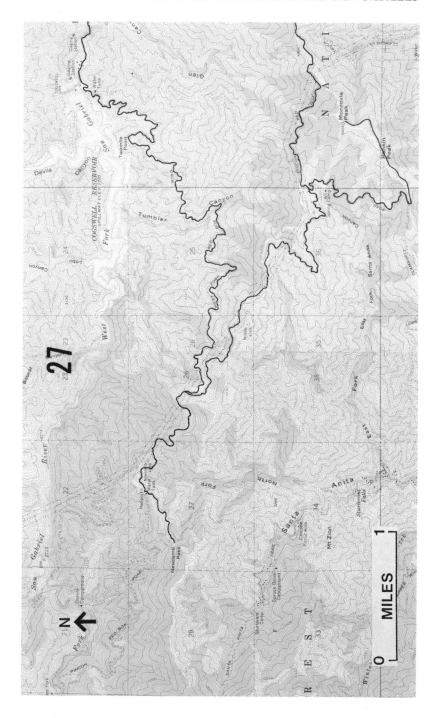

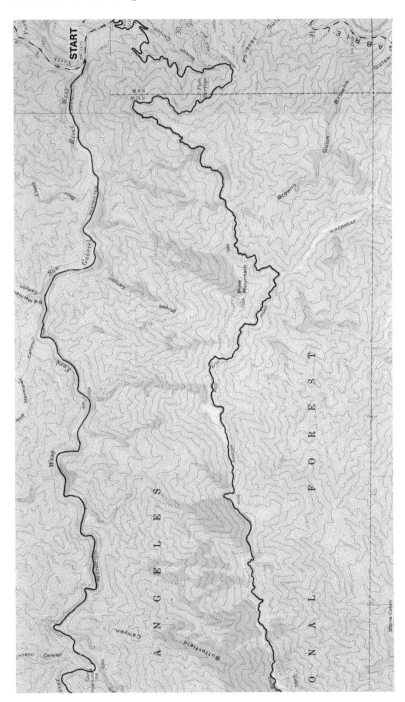

Trip 28

Iron Mountain

Distance: 11.20 miles
Time: 3 hours
Elevation gain: 1780 feet
Difficulty: Moderate
Topo: Chilao Flat
On the Hundred Peaks list

Take the recently paved Upper Big Tujunga Road either from the Angeles Crest Highway or the Angeles Forest Highway to a dirt road that takes off to the north exactly at milepost 3.50, at 3360 feet. The road is signed 4N18, and also warns of a ROUGH ROAD, but to me it's among the smoothest and best-maintained dirt roads in the Angeles Forest. In some places you are not even riding on dirt but directly over solid rock. You ford Lynx Creek twice and then at 1.22 miles you reach the first of several side roads that branch off to allow servicing of the electric towers. Not to worry—it's always easy to pick the main road. At 1.65 miles you go under the powerlines and see evidence of a recent fire on both sides of the road.

The first part of this trip is difficult and from the empty shells and cartridges that litter this road, future archeologists may conclude that this civilization did nothing but shoot.

As I was climbing, my eyes kept getting drawn to the sheer north side of Strawberry Peak (which from this perspective doesn't look very "strawberry-ish") and the impressive back side of Josephine Peak. At 3.75 miles, after 1¼ hours of climbing, you reach the road's summit. If you're a peak bagger, the rest of the way to Iron Mountain must be done on foot. If it makes you feel better, you can leave your bike chained to the electric tower. Climbing to the top, there is no actual trail—just keep going through the chaparral. After 25 hard minutes, you reach the 5040-foot summit. The trail register is in a Zip Lock bag under some rocks. Roundtop obscures your view of Pacifico Mountain, but most other peaks in the region can be seen.

Your descent down the chaparral-covered hill will take about 15 minutes. Back on your bike, you first drop and then climb to another summit at 4.13 miles. From the next downhill, you can see what appears to be either a junk yard or a dump. It is neither; it's the Black Cargo Mine. This and several other mines in the area were abandoned until a few years ago, when the price of gold was thought to have risen high enough to make its recovery profitable. There is no shortage of gold in the San Gabriels today, but its recovery is just too expensive to make it profitable. As you can see the fantasy of a gold mine may be romantic, but the reality is not.

At 4.83 miles you turn left and pass by the mine, then ford a tributary of Mill Creek several times. At 6.37 miles you reach the 3600-foot, 19-space Monte Cristo Campground, named after another mine in the area. Water and restrooms are here. Ride through the camp and then turn left onto Angeles Forest Highway. This paved road continues going downhill until you reach the Upper Big Tujunga Road at 7.74 miles. After a left turn, a series of rolling hills brings you back to your starting point at 11.20 miles, after 3 hours.

Sign posted throughout Arroyo Seco District

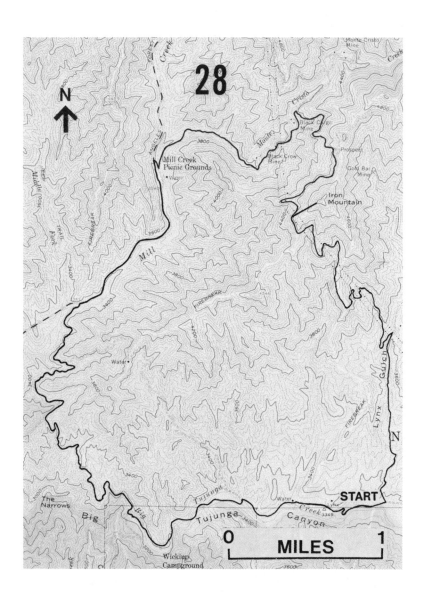

Rock formations on the way to Whittaker Peak

Trip 29

Perspiration Point Loop

Distance: 28.15 miles
Time: 6¼ hours
Elevation gain: 5200 feet
Difficulty: Strenuous
Topos: Acton, Agua Dulce, Condor Peak
Optional: Double water

In the first part of this century, some developers wanted to convert Mt. Gleason into a resort like Mt. Lowe or Mt. Wilson. In 1904 the prediction was made that it was "destined to be one of the great popular pleasure places on the coast." That never materialized, but in the 1950s a Nike missile base was built near the summit.

In the early 1970s, during the previous bike boom, the Mt. Gleason area was a cult destination. At that time the missile base was still operational, and the commanding officer allowed visitors to use its mess hall. Especially on a cold winter ride, with the snow freshly plowed onto the edges of the road, it was wonderful to be able to buy, at an elevation of over 1 mile, a warm meal and a cup of coffee . . . for about $1!

This ride begins 32 miles from La Canada at the end of the pavement on the Mt. Gleason Road at an elevation of 5600 feet. Don't take the paved road to the right that goes into the former Nike base, now a work camp that employs prisoners. Instead, you start riding down the dirt road that has no gate and is signed MT. GLEASON.

At mile 0.44 the dirt ends and you begin climbing on an excellent paved road. On the ridge to the right there is still barbed wire protecting part of the old Nike base. At 1.87 miles the narrow, gray, paved road, with its yellow line down the middle and Jeffrey pines on both sides, may remind you of riding in Yosemite.

At 2.52 miles, after 1 hour of climbing, you reach an AT&T microwave tower which from a distance resembles a fire lookout. At 2.56 miles a sign points left to the Messenger Flats and Lightning Point campgrounds. You'll go that way later, but now you turn right.

Immediately you reach the 6500-foot plateau of Mt. Gleason, which still has the support base for an old radar dome. It has been stripped and the ladder removed, but it's no challenge to an old rock climber. The view from the top is incredible: one of the best views in the San Gabriels. It would be a 360° view except that Waterman Mountain blocks a small area. You can see the entire San Gabriels, the Santa Monicas, the Ojai range, the Tehachapis, the southern Sierra Nevada, most of Antelope Valley, and even Muroc Dry Lake.

Unfortunately, because the road to here is paved, it is frequented not only by those who come to admire nature but also by those who come to party and then leave their cans, bottles and trash behind. At the west end of what used to be the parking lot for the radar dome are the remains of an old stone cabin. It appears to be as much a victim of vandalism as of decay. From here, you retrace your route back to a stop sign, where you turn right toward Messenger Flats.

After a fast descent between chaparral-covered hills that have been scarred by a fire, you turn right and leave the paved road at the next junction, signed MESSENGER FLATS CAMPGROUND 1. At 4.65 miles, after 1¼ hours, you reach the 5500-foot, 9-space Messenger Flats Campground, with piped water and pit toilets, a good spot for your first food break.

As you leave the campground, you may wonder whether you are in the mountains or the desert, as both pines and yuccas are present. At 5.07 miles you pass a road that goes to the summit of Messenger Peak, and then at 6.05 miles, where a SANTA CLARA DIVIDE ROAD sign is posted, you turn right and begin to lose altitude quickly.

At 9.76 miles you reach 4200-foot Perspiration Point, which is well named even though you are not climbing. A historical marker has been erected here. Although they have been removed by vandals, one side of the marker used to have a shovel and two picks. They implied that the marker is dedicated to the miners who played such a historical role in this area. But upon looking at the other side, you discover that, instead, it is dedicated to the Soledad CCC camp workers in 1934.

At 11.47 miles after 2¼ hours, you come to a 3500-foot junction, with 3 roads from which to choose. Take the one on the extreme left and begin climbing back into the mountains. At 12.37 miles Vasquez Rocks, a hideout of the bandit Tubercio Vasquez, stand out in the distance to your right.

Then at 17.00 miles, after 4 hours, you reach the 4,000-foot North Fork Station. You may think the climb has caused you to hallucinate because, just as on the Interstates, there is a roadside rest area with picnic tables, a drinking fountain, and a chemical toilet. It makes a good spot to recover from the climb.

You leave the North Fork area by the well-signed MESSENGER FLATS road. Although not a paved road, this is an easy climb, dominated by a view of Magic Mountain (the mountain, not the amusement park) off to your right. You're mostly using your middle chainwheel as you reach the junction at 20.67 miles, where you turn right. At 22.82 miles you reach the turnoff to Perspiration Point and at 24.28 miles you come to Messenger Flats Campground once more. At 25.12 miles you again reach the junction of the road to Lightning Point, where you turn left.

At 27.76 miles I don't know whether I was tired after 6 hours of riding or whether this paved road was really difficult, but I was in my lowest gear and wishing it were even lower. Even if clouds cover Los Angeles, one can usually see Catalina Island from here, and the slow pace also gives you time to notice the unusual perspective of being able to look down upon Mt. Wilson, Mt. Disappointment, Josephine Peak, Strawberry Peak and Mt. Lukens.

At 28.15 miles, after 6¼ hours of riding, you reach your starting point.

Perspiration Point

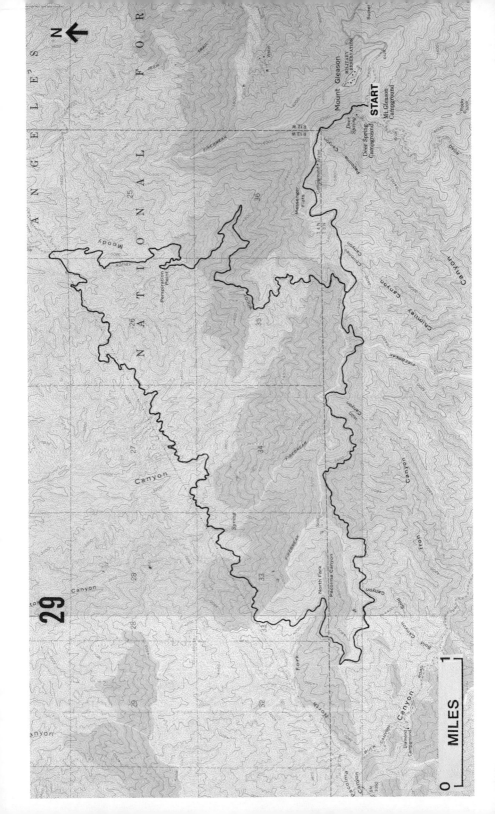

Trip 30

Pacoima Canyon Loop

Distance: 34.57 miles
Time: 9 hours
Elevation gain: 2910 feet
Difficulty: Strenuous
Topos: Acton, Agua Dulce, Condor Peak, Sunland
Optional: Double water

This ride begins 32 miles from La Canada at the end of the pavement on the Mt. Gleason Road at an elevation of 5600 feet. You don't want to take the paved road to the right that goes into the former Nike base. It's now a Conservation Camp that employs prisoners. Instead you start riding down the dirt road that has no gate and is signed MT. GLEASON.

At 3.13 miles you come to a **T** and turn left toward the Lightning Point Group Campground. The pavement immediately ends. At the junction at 6.54 miles you go left. At 6.91 miles is a spot from which Iron Mountain can be reached via a ridge, but I recommend continuing until at 8.19 miles the road reaches the other end of the ridge leading up to Iron Mountain.

I was unable to ride the bike up this ridge, but pushed it just far enough to be out of sight from the road and walked the remaining 0.12 mile to the top in about 15 minutes. From the 5635-foot summit, you can see the Mt. Gleason area, the entire front range, Big Tujunga Canyon and, even on many smoggy, hazy or foggy days, the tip of Catalina Island. Below you are Magic Mountain (the mountain, not the amusement park), the Piutes, and beyond them the southern Sierra Nevada.

At 14.14 miles you turn left onto the sideroad to Mendenhall Peak. This road hasn't been maintained since the fire-lookout tower was removed, and in many places shrubs have grown, leaving only a narrow trail. At 14.34 miles you come to the first of several short sections where most of the road has slid down the side of the hill.

At 15.17 miles, after 3 hours of riding, the 4636-foot summit of Mendenhall is reached. Not much remains of the tower that was destroyed in a fire storm. However, one morning on the top, I noticed a man's head pop up out of the old concrete water tank, much like a prairie dog out of his hole. This man, whom I nicknamed the Mendenhall Monk, is a Vietnam Vet who works in the canyon below and has cleverly and neatly converted the former tank into a camping spot.

He graciously invited me in, and as I sat on a bunk constructed from parts of the old tower, with his M-16 and his Bowie knife hanging from the wall, he fixed some delicious pancakes for us. As we ate, he talked of his experiences in the war and we listened to some New Wave music on his radio.

At 16.18 miles you again reach the main road, and then continue your descent. At 18.08 miles, at a junction directly under the powerlines, you go right. At 21.03 miles and an elevation of 2960 feet, you are now riding through upper Pacoima Canyon. In the spring this can be a wet ride, but later in the summer it is bone dry. You frequently cross the streambed as you continue up the canyon. Next you come to a car that has been "lightened" by target shooters. Another thing that detracts from the beauty of this canyon is that shotgun shells have seemingly rained onto the road.

At 22.00 miles you keep right, then at 22.49 miles take the road that goes uphill. Since it follows the streambed, this is a gradual, easy climb. At 24.33 miles you bear left and begin the climb out of the canyon. Then, at 26.34 miles, you reach the 400-foot North Fork Station and the North Fork Roadside Rest Area. The latter has picnic tables, water, and a chemical toilet.

At 33.69 miles you reach Messenger Flats and at 34.57 miles and 9 hours you reach the start.

"Lightened" 1964 Cadillac in Pacoima Canyon

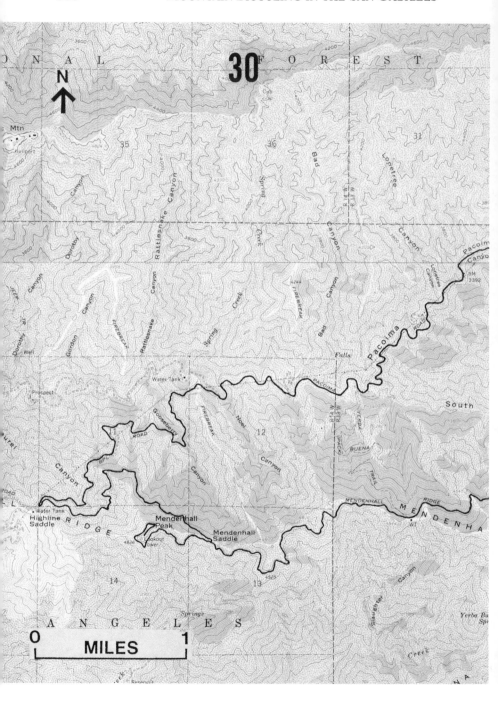

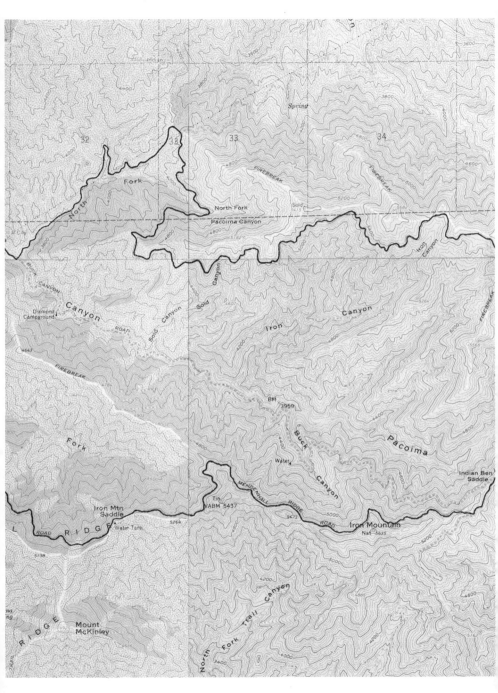

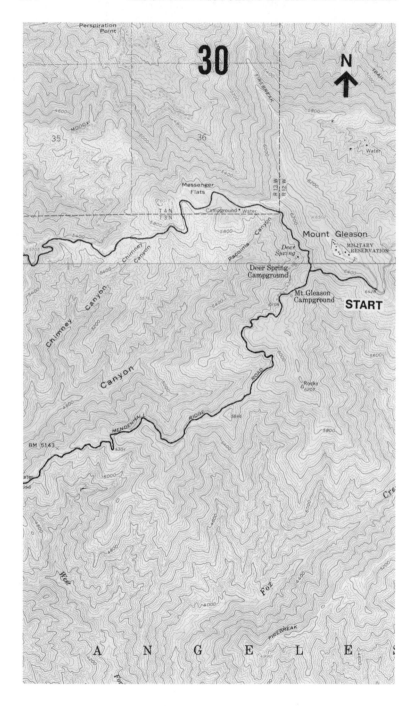

Trip 31

Magic Mountain

Distance: 31.05 miles
Time: 6¼ hours
Elevation gain: 2937 feet
Difficulty: Strenuous
Topos: Agua Dulce, San Fernando, Sunland
Optional: Double water
Note: Not recommended on weekends or holidays because of target shooters.

This ride begins at the 2800-foot Bear Divide Vista, at the junction of Little Tujunga Canyon Road and Sand Canyon Road. (Note: although maps show this as Bear Canyon Road, it is signed SAND CANYON.) You begin riding along the Sand Canyon Road, but almost immediately, at mile 0.10, you turn right and start the easy climb up paved Santa Clara Divide Road 3N17. Even in late September, after a rainless summer, it is lined with white and yellow wildflowers.

At 2.34 miles, after about 30 minutes of climbing, you come to a small grove of pine and fir trees. To get a better view, you need to ride about 20 feet off the pavement to a saddle. From this saddle, stretched out before you are Mt. Gleason, Iron Mountain, Mendenhall Peak, Mt. Lukens, the Verdugo hills and, winding far below you, Little Tujunga Road. Unfortunately, the wilderness experience is usually marred by the sounds of gunfire echoing up from Pacoima Canyon.

Return to the pavement, descend, and at 2.97 miles begin climbing the flanks of Magic Mountain. At 6.51 miles, after 1½ hours of climbing, you reach the junction to Magic Mountain. Turn left onto the paved road, carry your bike around the usually locked gate, and reach 4785-foot Magic Mountain at 7.07 miles after 1¾ hours. Another former Nike missile base, it must have been one of the first to be dismantled, as even a 1967 book describes it as an "abandoned" missile base.

The remains of this base are some of the most elaborate in the San Gabriels. There is no actual "summit," so to get a 360° view you have to walk completely around the twin, rusting water tanks and the fenced-off microwave tower that occupy Magic Mountain today. Doing so gives you a good view of the Canyon Country, Mt. Gleason, the tip of Strawberry Peak, Mt. Lukens, Mendenhall Peak, the San Fernando Valley, the Santa Monica Mountains, and Santa Susana Pass.

From Magic Mountain the entire front range of the San Gabriels is hidden. A newcomer to the area would probably not realize that Mt. Wilson, Waterman Mountain, or even Mt. Baldy existed.

Coming down off Magic Mountain, you must again dismount to get around the gate. At 7.57 miles you turn left and leave the pavement. You continue descending, making another left at 9.30 miles, and at 10.18 miles come to the junction with 4N37, signed INDIAN CANYON. Here you keep going straight and encounter a hard climb of almost one mile. The road then drops, climbs, and drops again until at 14.53 miles, after more than 3 hours of riding, you reach 4,000-foot North Fork Station.

After using the picnic tables, shade, water fountain and toilet of the station's rest area, you leave the North Fork region by taking the road signed LITTLE TUJUNGA CANYON ROAD 11 MI. At 15.42 miles you enter Pacoima Canyon and make the first of the trip's many stream crossings.

In several ways this canyon reminds me of the Arroyo Seco. It has a road that parallels, crosses, recrosses, and sometimes goes down the middle of a stream. It has impressive granite walls. In the spring or after a storm, the sound of water cascading over rocks can be heard. But it also has shaded quiet spots.

Unlike in the Arroyo, shooting is allowed, and the road is open to motor vehicles—some capable of the journey, some not. As a result, the natural peace of the canyon has been violated. Therefore, I can recommend this trip only on weekdays. The amount of gunfire on an ordinary weekend made me anxious. I'm sure it would terrify many cyclists.

On the other hand, it's sometimes eye-opening and necessary to see first-hand the results of allowing anything and everything that doesn't move (and probably many things that do) to become a target; to see the results of tons of shells, bullets and cans being brought into an area without any being removed; and to see how disrespect for the environment and the rights and values of others can turn a quiet canyon into a battlefield.

It would also be an interesting location to set up a meeting between pro- and anti-mountain-bicycle forces. Compared to the targetshooters, the mountain bicyclist might seem harmless.

At 16.44 miles you angle right and continue to follow the Pacoima, and at 20.02 miles you come across the first of a handful of abandoned vehicles, a 1964 Cadillac that has been "lightened" courtesy of the local target shooters.

The road appears to end at 20.75 miles, but you meet up with it again by riding through the middle of the streambed for about 100 feet. At 22.85 miles you reach the remains of an abandoned titanium mine which have been converted into Swiss cheese by bullets. It makes you wonder whether this canyon has been eroded by nature or simply blown away.

At 23.11 miles the road ahead looks as if it crossed the stream and climbed, but instead it goes right. At 24.42 miles you again ride in the middle of the streambed for a short distance.

By now, on a typical weekend, you are encountering an enormous amount of gunfire—so much that the old Dutch Louie Campground has been abandoned. But you can still see the old tunnel that Dutch Louie, the miner, built to divert the stream. Near it is another car riddled with bullets, this time a Continental. Apparently, high-income people come here to abandon their cars.

At 25.25 miles, after crossing the stream 67 times, you at last begin the difficult climb out of the canyon. At 26.40 miles you reach the summit, and go right. Then, at 26.80 miles and 2700 feet, you reach the pavement of Little Tujunga Canyon Road.

Now you begin a fast, paved, curved descent. If your tire pressure was low enough for the sand and rocks of Pacoima Canyon, they now probably will feel as if they were going to roll off the rims. At 29.35 miles you pay for the fun of having dropped down to 2200 feet by starting the climb back to Bear Divide. At 29.78 miles, at milepost 9.45, you reach the Earthquake Fault Picnic Area. It has one table, one stove, a sign explaining the earthquakes of the region, and a short trail that allows a close inspection of the San Gabriel Fault.

At 31.05 miles, after 6¼ hours of riding, you reach Bear Divide Vista. As you drink some water from the fountain, you can read the sign that tells of Don Gaspar de Portola's 1769 journey through California.

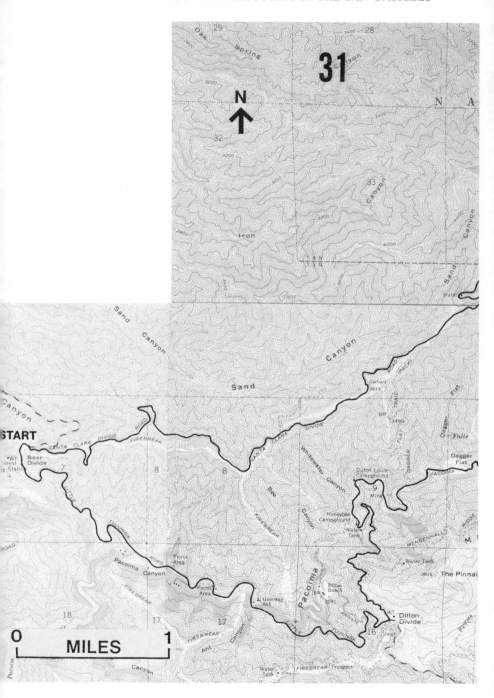

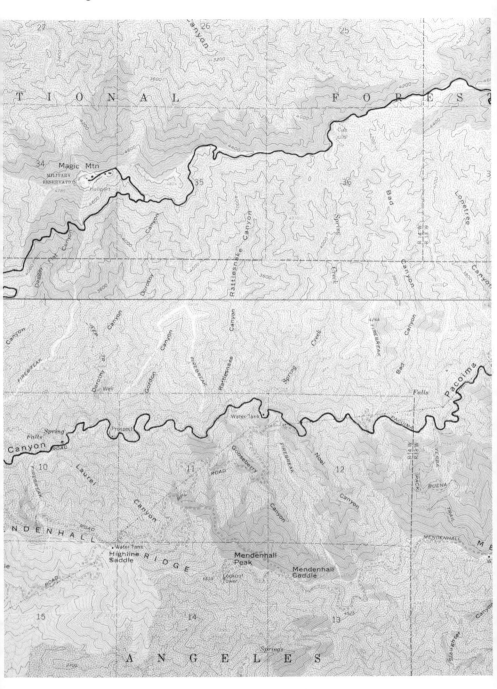

Trip 32

Mount Gleason–Tujunga Canyon Loop

Distance: 29.95 miles
Time: 6½ hours
Elevation gain: 3442 feet
Difficulty: Strenuous
Topos: Acton, Chilao Flat, Condor Peak
Optional: Double water
On the Hundred Peaks list

This loop starts at an elevation of 3242 feet at the junction of Big Tujunga Canyon Road and Angeles Forest Highway, at milepost 21.09. The first mile is mostly downhill; then at 2800 feet and 2.53 miles you cross Big Tujunga on a modern-looking bridge that was actually built in 1941. A castlelike walkway goes out for a short distance on the north side. At 2.91 miles you enter a tunnel, the most hazardous part of the trip. I recommend that you wait for a break in traffic and then sprint through. Fortunately, the road going through the tunnel is level. At 2.98 miles, just after you leave the tunnel, is Hidden Springs Picnic Ground. It's well worth the short hike down from the parking lot to see some of the prettiest pools in the San Gabriels.

Hidden Springs Cafe, the only "civilization" on this ride, is at 3.31 miles. Next you pass the Monte Cristo Fire Station; the junction with Upper Big Tujunga Canyon Road; the 3,600-foot Monte Cristo Campground, with 19 spaces, water, and pit toilets; and Baughman Springs, with some pretty stone seats, but a usually capped drinking fountain.

At 10.41 miles, after 1¾ hours of climbing, you top 4900-foot Mill Creek Summit. The picnic area here is a good place to get some water and fill your bottles. It also has pit toilets. Leaving the picnic area, you cross Angeles Forest Highway and begin the rugged climb up Mt. Gleason Road. At 11.08 miles, framed through

Jeffrey pines, firs and oaks, you get your first view of Antelope Valley. In this region you can also hear, sometimes once an hour, sonic booms from the aircraft being tested at Edwards Air Force Base.

Since Mill Creek summit you've been paralleling the Pacific Crest Trail. It now crosses the road for the first of several times. From here you have a clear view of the range from Pacifico Mountain to Mt. Lukens.

At 16.34 miles, after 2¾ hours of climbing, the road reaches the 5600-foot saddle just below Mt. Gleason (see Trip 29). The paved road curves to the right and enters the former missile base, now a conservation camp. Although it's accessible, the public is asked to stay out because the camp does use prisoners. There are also two dirt roads that lead off from this spot. One is signed MT. GLEASON, the other is unsigned and has a locked gate. You take the latter.

Basically, the road drops, but it does make 3 climbs before it reaches Big Tujunga Canyon. At 17.08 miles you have an excellent view of Vetter Mountain, Mt. Wilson, Strawberry Peak, Josephine Peak, and Mt. Lukens.

At 19.32 and at 20.49 miles you ford small creeks, and then, at 21.71 miles, reach a high point from which you can see the junction of Tujunga Canyon Road and Angeles Forest Highway. It looks close, but it is still almost 10 hard miles away. The road here is sandy, and even downhill travel is work.

You cross another small creek before you reach the bottom of the canyon at 27.60 miles. The cool waters of the Big Tujunga are great for soaking hot, tired feet before the final, difficult climb out of the canyon. At 29.28 miles, after a road section that required some walking, you reach Big Tujunga Canyon Road. After a left turn and another 10 minutes of easy climbing, you are at your starting place after 29.95 miles.

Descending Pacifico Mountain

32

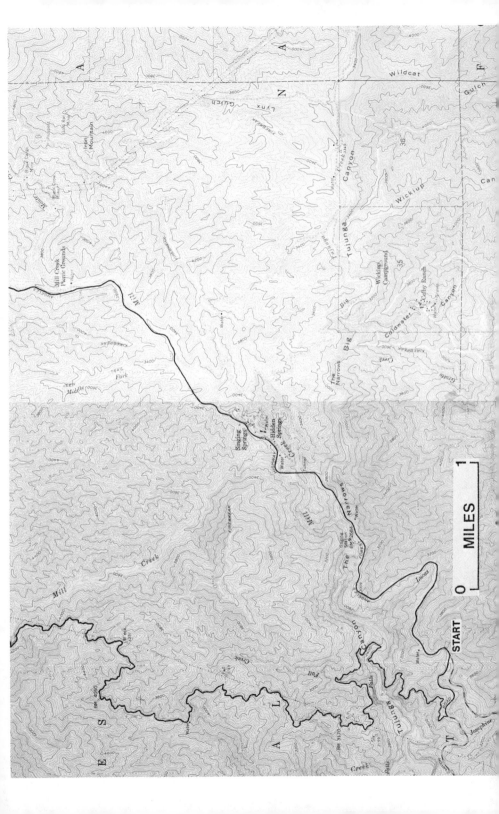

START

MILES
0   1

Trip 33

Pacifico Mountain

Distance: 18.18 miles
Time: 5 hours
Elevation gain: 2340 feet
Difficulty: Moderate
Topos: Chilao Flat, Pacifico Mountain
Optional: Double water
On the Hundred Peaks list

To reach the start take Angeles Forest Highway to 4900-foot Mill Creek Summit. The ride begins from the Mill Creek Picnic Area, whose drinking fountain is the trip's only source of water. Turn right and go past the ranger station and residences to a parking lot. Two dirt roads leave the parking lot. Take the gated, northern one. Motorcycles can also ride around this locked gate, so you should be on the lookout for them.

After riding through the Penny Pines Program's Mill Creek Plantation, you begin to see the Mojave Desert behind you and Josephine Peak, Mt. Lukens and Mt. Gleason in front. Then at 1.85 miles the Mojave bursts into view again, with the red Piute Mountains and the southern Sierra also visible on a clear day. At a junction at 3.08 miles you take the road signed MT. PACIFICO CAMPGROUND 3 MI.

From this road you can see in the valley below the three forks of Alder Creek, the Loomis Ranch (the most distant of the Great Hiking Era's resorts), and in the distance beyond this valley, Mt. Wilson. After riding through some spectacular granite formations, you turn left onto the unsigned road to Pacifico at 4.75 miles. At 4.94 miles you bear right and then at 6.27 miles, after 2 hours, you reach Upper Pacifico Campground.

Among huge granite boulders and underneath enormous Jeffrey pines that have covered the ground with their cones, the waterless,

7-space, 7100-foot campground offers breathtaking views of
Antelope Valley. To the north are the Mojave Desert, Lake
Palmdale and Little Rock Reservoir. The gigantic, easily spotted
hangar is the Rockwell plant, where the space shuttles were built.
To the east you can see as far as Mt. Baldy.

On the way out, you reach the main road at 7.80 miles and
follow it until at 6200 feet and after 9.08 miles, you turn left onto
the route signed ROUND TOP ROAD 3N90. At 9.90 miles you reach
6100-foot Roundtop Campground. Actually built on the edge of
Granite Mountain, it has 4 spaces but lacks water. Although it's not
as pretty as Upper Pacifico, it does offer views of the Mojave
Desert, Mt. Gleason, Waterman Mountain and Vetter Mountain.

At 12.09 miles 6316-foot Round Top is reached. From here,
you can see Waterman Mountain, Pacifico Mountain, Vetter Mountain, Mt. Wilson, Mt. Disappointment, Josephine Peak, Mt.
Gleason, and Mt. Lukens.

On your return, go left at the junction at 15.10 miles and reach
the start at 18.18 miles.

The author

Michelle Immler

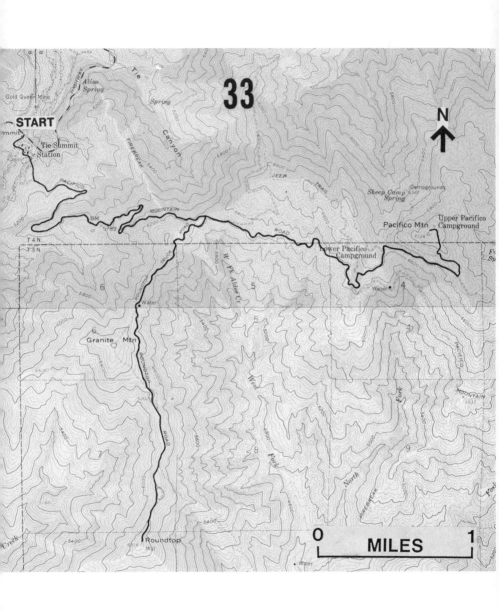

Trip 34

Whittaker Peak

Distance: 9.91 miles
Time: 2 hours
Elevation gain: 1560 feet
Difficulty: Easy to moderate
Topo: Whittaker Peak

To reach the start of this ride, take Interstate 5 north from Los Angeles beyond Lake Castaic to the Templin Highway exit. Turn left, and then immediately turn right onto the old Ridge Route, now known as the Golden State Highway. Just 1½ miles along this road, park across from the WHITTAKER PEAK 4 MILES sign.

Before you begin the climb, notice that there are two sides to the sign. The southern side reads 4 MILES but its northern counterpart gives the distance as 4½ MILES. Start from the northern side only if you feel up to the additional 1 mile round trip!

From the 2760-foot start, you climb primarily through chaparral, although there are also yuccas, oaks and, in spring and early summer, wildflowers, including lilacs. The first mile is a paved climb from which you can see the old Ridge Route that brought you to the start. Just beyond, you can see the newest Ridge Route, Interstate 5. And over the next hill beyond it, you can spot, on a ridge, the *original* Ridge Route. Then, as the road levels off, you turn a corner and leave the noise from the Interstate behind. Keep going right at the sign WHITAKER PEAK 3.

At 1.94 miles, as the pavement disappears, you ride through a formation that reminds me of Vasquez Rocks. At a **Y** in the road, turn onto the left branch. The pavement reappears and you descend until, at 2.41 miles, the pavement deteriorates and you begin climbing again.

At 3.10 miles round a bend and see the telephone microwave towers near the peak. After 4.43 miles and one hour of climbing, you reach the 4120-foot summit, just beyond the towers. You are surrounded by mountains. The Sespe Condor Sanctuary is just over the ridge to the west, and below you and to the southwest are Lake Piru, Piru Creek, and the smaller bodies of water that supply it.

On the way back, there is a climb between 6.46 and 6.91 miles. At the top of this climb, turn left, and from there to 7.42 miles you can better explore the rock formation that runs through this area.

From this spot you retrace your route to reach the start at 9.91 miles, after a little over two hours of riding.

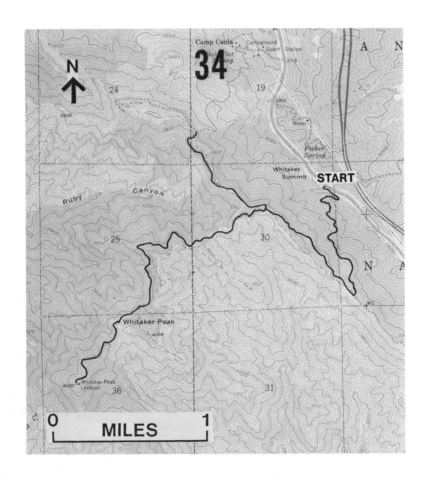

Associations

National Off-Road Bicycle Association. Box 1901, Chandler, AZ 85924.

NORBA is more involved in racing than in touring, and they have just undergone a change in ownership. However, they are the only game in town.

Sierra Club, Angeles Chapter, 2410 Beverly Blvd., Los Angeles, California, 90057.

Although the National Sierra Club has expressed an opposition to mountain bikes (to protest this, at my last renewal, I downgraded my membership from family to regular), the club's Angeles Chapter's Bicycle Touring Committee is the *only* organization that currently leads group mountain-bike rides into the San Gabriels.

References and Suggested Readings

All-Terrain Bikes. Rodale Press, Emmaus, PA, 1985.

Cunningham, Richard. "Back Country Touring." Mountain Bike Action, July 1986.

Fulford, D. G. "Whose Woods These Are." Altadena Weekly, September 18, 1986.

Hillsbery, Kief. "Riding High." *Backpacker,* July, 1985

Katz, Jesse. "Riders Resist the Wheel." Los Angeles Times, November 3, 1985.

Kelly, Charles. "Riding Styles for the Wilds: Off-Road Technique." Bicycling (June 1982) 110–111.

Leadabrand, Russ. *A Guidebook to the Mountains of Southern California.* Ward Ritchie Press, Los Angeles, 1967.

Miller, Jeffrey. "Happy Trails." *Los Angeles Times,* July 24, 1986.

Oates, Stephen B. *To Purge This Land With Blood: A Biography of John Brown.* Harper & Row, New York, 1970.

Robinson, John W. *Mines of the San Gabriels.* La Siesta Press, Glendale, CA, 1973.

Robinson, John W. *The San Gabriels: Southern California Mountain Country.* Golden West Books, San Marino, CA, 1977.

Robinson, John W. *The San Gabriels II: The Mountains from Monrovia Canyon to Lytle Creek.* Big Santa Anita Historical Society, 1983.

Robinson, John W. *Trails of the Angeles: 100 hikes in the San Gabriels.* Wilderness Press, Berkeley, 1986.

Sanders, William. "Biking Back Roads." Bicycling (May 1981) 61.

Seims, Charles. *Mount Lowe: The Railway in the Clouds.* Golden West Books, San Marino, 1976.

Slack-Elliott, Chuck. "Cycling Forgotten Roads." Bicycling (May, 1981) 58.

Watts, Tom. *Pacific Coast Tree Finder.* Nature Study Guild, Berkeley, 1973.

Wilson, Larry. "Bikers will be educated in dirt-road techniques." Altadena Weekly (March 13, 1986).

The all-terrain bicycle has liberated the cyclotourist! No longer will we be relegated to a few ribbons of pavement to guide us past the natural wonders we seek to experience. Paved roads lead to cities, dirt roads and trails lead to places. The instant [the] bicycle leaves the pavement, we become intimately involved with the terrain. We taste the dust, feel the texture of gravel and rocky creeks, mud and sand roll beneath our wheels. We begin to sense the geographical changes as they unfold before us. We become explorers instead of tourists, fueled by the anticipation of what places lie ahead.

When we rejoin the pavement, we are shocked by the sounds and smells of motorized humanity, but we are relieved by how smooth the highway is and the fact that restaurants and showers won't be too far ahead.... This is what all-terrain bicycles were created for—to take you nearly everywhere on the map, not just where the bold lines go ...

—Richard Cunningham, *Mountain Bike Action,* July 1986

Index